WHY BLACKS LEFT
AMERICA FOR AFRICA

WHY BLACKS LEFT AMERICA FOR AFRICA

Interviews with Black Repatriates, 1971–1999

Robert Johnson, Jr.

Westport, Connecticut
London

Library of Congress Cataloging-in-Publication Data

Johnson, Robert.
    Why Blacks left America for Africa : interviews with Black
repatriates, 1971–1999 / Robert Johnson, Jr.
        p.   cm
    Includes bibliographical references and index.
    ISBN 0–275–96595–3 (alk. paper)
    1. Afro-Americans—Africa, East Interviews.   2. Immigrants—
Africa, East Interviews.   3. Africa, East—Emigration and
immigration.   4. United States—Emigration and immigration.
I. Title.
DT429.5.A38J65   1999
304.8′3676073—dc21   98–56072

British Library Cataloguing in Publication Data is available.

Library of Congress Catalog Card Number: 98–56072
ISBN: 0–275–96595–3

First published in 1999

Praeger Publishers, 88 Post Road West, Westport, CT 06881
An imprint of Greenwood Publishing Group, Inc.
www.praeger.com

Printed in the United States of America

The paper used in this book complies with the
Permanent Paper Standard issued by the National
Information Standards Organization (Z39.48–1984).

10 9 8 7 6 5 4 3 2 1

This book is dedicated to my children:
Anika Ama Johnson and Gary Weldon Johnson,
the strength of my life.

Contents

Preface

This book is an examination of the reasons why a group of Black Americans left the United States for Africa between 1971 and 1999. The stories revealed here are personal, revealing compelling individual explanations for the decision to repatriate to Africa.

The interviews are, by necessity, from East Africa because it was during 1971–1972 that I lived there as a result of a Thomas J. Watson Fellowship. It was my second trip to Africa; the first trip was in 1968, when I lived for eight weeks in civil war–torn Nigeria. On the second trip, I came into contact with fellow Americans who had left America. It was there that I decided to interview as many individuals as I could. For the most part, the interviews were in Kenya and Tanzania, though I did spend considerable time with individuals in Uganda and Ethiopia.

For the past twenty-eight years, I have been pondering the question of whether African-Americans consider themselves to be primarily American or African. This is an issue that was addressed by other scholars, most notably, the late historian W.E.B. Du Bois in his pioneering work of the last century, *The Souls of Black Folk*. He described the conflict as "two souls, two thoughts, two unreconciled strivings; two warring ideals in one dark body, whose dogged strength alone keeps it from being torn asunder."[1]

Nevertheless, many African-Americans have taken the ultimate step of leaving America and returning to Africa. This limited study is a glimpse at the lives of some of these brave pioneers. It is not intended to be a scientific investigation of repatriation activities during this period, but rather, a narrative of recent life experiences in the latter part of the twentieth century. Most of the names have been changed, but not the content of the interviews.

I am very grateful to the Thomas J. Watson Foundation for its support during an early phase in my career. Without the travel fellowship, I never would have met the extraordinary people in this book. I also thank Maria Veiga-Taylor for her untiring assistance in typing the initial draft from the discolored, flimsy notes that had lingered in my files for over twenty years. I especially appreciate the untiring effort of Nikeiya Mitchell, a senior at University of Massachusetts Boston, who prepared the manuscript for submission to the publisher. Her professionalism has meant that the work was presented in its best form. Finally, I thank my wife, Amy Merrill, for her comments on the introduction and conclusion.

NOTE

1. W.E.B. Du Bois, *The Souls of Black Folk* (Greenwich, Conn.: Fawcett Publications, 1961), 17.

Introduction

In the twentieth century, more than any other time in American history, we saw the rise of massive Black conceived and supported repatriation initiatives. Most well known was the Marcus Garvey Movement, which began in Jamaica in 1914, was brought to America in 1916, and continues to the present day under the leadership of Marcus Garvey Jr. Years later, as more African-Americans became exposed to Black nationalist ideologies in the 1970s and 1980s, interest in Africa began to develop rapidly among individuals.

Repatriation did not have its genesis in the twentieth century. Rather, it stretches back to the earliest slave ships when Africans found themselves bound for a foreign land and struggled to escape and make their way back home. Viewed in that context, it is the oldest expression of Black nationalism.

It was not, however, until the nineteenth century that Africans were able to return to Africa as part of any organizational efforts. Repatriation in the nineteenth century occurred primarily through the efforts of the American Colonization Society, but Black nationalist and revolutionary efforts were also instrumental. Under the leadership of Cinque, kidnapped Africans on the ship *Amistad* not only mutinied, but also demanded that they be taken back to Africa. This slave ship revolt occurred in 1839, and the Africans continued their struggles in the American courts until they were allowed to return to Africa in 1841 (*United States v.* Amistad, 40 U.S. 518 [1841]).

PAUL CUFFE (1759–1817)

Repatriation of free Blacks in the nineteenth century had its birth in a movement organized and financed by a remarkable African-American, Paul Cuffe. In 1815, Cuffe resettled thirty-eight Africans in the British colony of Sierra Leone. He believed that the repatriates would have a positive impact upon Africa by converting the African population to Christianity and developing commerce between Liberia and America. Cuffe was born to free parents in Westport, Massachusetts, on January 17, 1759. Cuffe Slocum, his father, a native of Ghana, purchased his freedom in 1728.[1] Young Cuffe began working on whaling ships in 1775; by 1781, he had built his own ship and gathered an all African crew in preparation for his journey to Sierra Leone.

When Cuffe and his crew of nine Black men and one Swede arrived in Sierra Leone on March 1, 1811, they understood the importance of maintaining a cordial relationship both with the British colonials who controlled the country and the Africans. Cuffe was greeted by the governor of the colony, yet he insisted upon meeting with African rulers and their people.

After preparing the groundwork for his repatriation effort, Cuffe returned to the United States to garner more support. On December 4, 1815, he, his crew, and thirty-eight passengers set sail for Sierra Leone. On February 3, 1816, they touched African soil, making history as the first Africans to return to the continent from America through their own financial resources. These pioneers, from New York City, Philadelphia, and Boston, joined Cuffe's voyage because they believed in the importance of returning to Africa and building a nation. Each volunteered to leave America and to pay for the cost of their passage, which ranged from one hundred to two hundred fifty dollars per person.[2]

WHITE RESETTLEMENT EFFORTS

However, even before Cuffe made his voyage to Africa, white politicians in America had been seriously debating the removal of Blacks from the country. In 1777, a committee of the Virginia legislature, which was chaired by Thomas Jefferson, debated the merits of emancipation in order to send Blacks to Africa. Other prominent American patriots, who supported plans to remove Blacks from the United States, were Abraham Lincoln and Henry Clay. During the Civil War, when the nation was divided over the question of slavery and Black integration into American society, Lincoln asked the Congress of the United States to allocate funds for the settlement of free Africans in Central America.[3] Two American presidents, George Washington and William Howard Taft, encouraged free Blacks to emigrate to Africa. President Grant worked diligently after the Civil War to annex Santo Domingo for the resettlement of Africans living in America.[4]

These resettlement efforts on the part of prominent American political leaders reflected both the racism of the times and the economic justification for Black removal. The free Black population was increasing rapidly, and many politicians saw it as a threat to the economic viability of the plantation system. For example, in the year 1775, Africans comprised 40 percent of Virginia's population and over 30 percent of the population of North Carolina and Georgia. This growth of the Black population in America greatly alarmed the White population, who, for the most part, felt that it was inconceivable for a race of people, who were considered by even the clergy to be innately inferior to the White race, to live among them. Therefore, resettlement to Africa was a means to rid America of a despised class of people.

AMERICAN COLONIZATION SOCIETY

One year after Paul Cuffe took thirty-eight African-Americans to Sierra Leone, the American Colonization Society was formed in Washington, D.C. Its first president was Bushrod Washington, brother of President George Washington, who favored the resettlement of Africans. Henry Clay, the founding secretary of the Society, advocated the extermination of Native Americans and had the following to say about Africans in America:

Can there be a nobler cause than that which, whilst it proposed to rid our country of a useless and pernicious, if not dangerous portion of our population, contemplates the spreading of civilized life, and the possible redemption from ignorance and barbarism of a benighted quarter of the globe?[5]

For most of the nineteenth century, the American Colonization Society controlled resettlement efforts to Africa. It is also clear that the founders of the new society did not have the best interests of African-Americans at heart. Rather, the American government saw resettlement as a means of eliminating from the American population a group who constituted a potential threat to those in power, and the White industrialists saw removal of free African-Americans as the elimination of competitive labor and of a threat to the plantation system.

JOHN BROWN RUSSWURM (1799–1851)

Free Blacks during the nineteenth century were divided over resettlement. Some, such as Paul Cuffe, John Brown Russwurm, and Lott Cary, actively supported resettlement schemes, whereas others, such as Frederick Douglass; unequivocally fought the efforts of the American Colonization Society. However, many Blacks, who did remain in America, identified themselves with Africa. Many chose to refer to themselves as "African" as in the case of the Free African Society, the African Aid Society, and the African Methodist Episcopal Church.

Of all the free Blacks in the nineteenth century, Russwurm was the most pragmatic in that he used the White colonization society as a vehicle for achieving his nationalist ends. His reversal of position, editorials in support of colonization, and decision in 1829 to repatriate under the auspices of the Society caused tremendous uproar among free African-Americans. His effigy was even burned in the five corners section of New York City, where most of the "coloreds" lived. Yet for Russwurm, Liberia represented promise and an opportunity for talented African-Americans to rise to the highest levels of political leadership.

Russwurm was born in Port Antonio, Jamaica, on October 1, 1799. His father, John Russwurm, was a wealthy Virginia planter, and his mother, Eliza, a Jamaican concubine.[6] In 1807, young Russwurm was sent by his father to Quebec, where he was privately educated before rejoining his father in Portland, Maine, in 1813. From 1813 to 1819, young Russwurm was enrolled at Hebron Academy, one of the finest private schools in the District of Maine. After graduating in 1819, he moved to Boston, where he became principal of the Primus Hall School, which had been established by free Blacks. In 1824, he began his junior year at Bowdoin College, graduating in 1826.

By the time he graduated, he had developed a clear perspective on the need for Blacks to violently oppose colonialism. His commencement speech, given on September 12, 1826, applauded the revolutionary goals of the Haitian Revolution. In a stirring speech, which was the earliest Pan-African revolutionary speech by an African-American college student, Russwurm warned the nation that self-determination could never be stifled forever:

It is in the irresistible course of events that all men, who have been deprived of their liberty, shall recover this precious portion of their indefeasible inheritance. It is in vain to stem the current; degraded man will rise in his majesty, and claim his right. They may be withheld from him now, but the day will arrive, when they must be surrendered.[7]

He made his unpopular decision to repatriate in September 1829 for many reasons, despite his prominent role as cofounder and editor of the first Black newspaper, *Freedom's Journal*. The major reason, however, was his belief that there was not much of a future for Africans in America. In Liberia, he served in the positions of superintendent of Monrovia's schools and editor of the *Liberia Herald*. Russwurm served as an employee of the American Colonization Society until 1836, when he and his wife, Sarah (McGill) Russwurm, moved with their children to Cape Palmas Colony, where he served as governor until his death in 1851. No other Black nationalist of the nineteenth century could boast of such a successful return to the continent.

BISHOP HENRY McNEAL TURNER (1834–1915)

By 1892, after the Society ceased its active involvement with Liberia the outspoken Bishop Henry McNeal Turner of the African Methodist Episcopal Church assumed a leadership role in marshaling support for repatriation. Bishop Turner was born on February 1, 1834, in Newberry, South Carolina. Like Cuffe, he had been born to free parents. From the end of the Civil War into the twentieth century, Turner was the leading supporter of repatriation.

Despite the promises of a new life after the Civil War, most Blacks found themselves abandoned by the federal government and northern carpetbaggers. Bishop Turner joined a chorus of individuals and groups who supported repatriation to Africa. Some of the organizations that sprang into existence included the Kansas African Emigration Association (1887) and the Liberia Exodus Company, founded by Martin Delany and Bishop Turner. The latter organization bought a ship and transported two hundred Blacks to Liberia.[8] Other noteworthy attempts included that of Dr. Alpert Thone, who attempted to transport Blacks to the Belgian Congo in 1915, but failed, and Alfred C. Sam, from the Gold Coast, who raised $100,000 in Kansas and Oklahoma and transported sixty Blacks to Liberia in his ship, *The Liberia* in 1915.[9] After Turner heard Alexander Crummell, another advocate of repatriation, speak, he began to integrate repatriation into his sermons and openly advocated the African return. He wrote:

The Negro race has as much chance in the U.S. . . . of being a man . . . as a frog has in a snake den. . . . Emigrate and gradually return to the land of our ancestors. . . . The Negro was brought here in the providence of God to learn obedience, to work, to sing, to pray, to preach, acquire education, deal with mathematical abstractions and imbibe the principles of civilization as a whole, and then to return to Africa, the land of his fathers, and bring her his millions.[10]

On May 14, 1880, he was elected to the bishophood with 66 percent of the vote.[11] This margin of victory signaled that the church was willing to endorse many of the repatriation ideas that Turner had adopted five years earlier.

By the end of the century, the socioeconomic condition of Blacks had deteriorated. Lynching was prevalent throughout the South, and Bishop Turner spoke out against such atrocities. Between 1883 and 1899, 2,500 Blacks were lynched. In the first years of the new century and before the beginning of the First World War, 1,100 Blacks met the same fate.[12] It is reported that in 1917 in Tennessee, 3,000 whites came out to see what was advertised as the burning of a "live Negro."[13] In 1891, the Council of Bishops authorized Turner to take an exploratory trip to Africa. In February 1892, he returned not only determined to establish missions in Africa, but also to repatriate African-Americans. His plan was to repatriate 5 to 10 million Blacks per year. He had hoped that wealthy Blacks and the federal government would provide financial assistance.[14] The U.S. government, he argued, owed reparations of about $40 billion for the free service Blacks had provided the country for 200 years.

In his appeal to the working-class poor, Turner's philosophy foreshadowed that of Marcus Garvey. The genius of Bishop Turner stemmed from his undying love for African people and his firm belief that for Africans to be respected, they had to become a nation.

REPATRIATION IN THE TWENTIETH CENTURY: MARCUS GARVEY

Repatriation movements in the twentieth century took on a clear Pan-African perspective under the leadership of Bishop Turner and Marcus Garvey. The fundamental difference between the movements of the nineteenth and twentieth centuries was that the latter was, for the most part, mass based. Nineteenth-century Black nationalist leaders, such as John B. Russwurm, Lott Cary, and Sarah McGill,[15] came from privileged backgrounds, whereas leaders in the twentieth century came from the Black poor. Under his Universal Negro Improvement Association, which was incorporated in the United States on July 2, 1918, Marcus Garvey sought as his goal "[t]he establishment of a central nation for Black people."[16] By 1925, he had established 996 branches in the United States and around the world, with a membership of over 2 million.[17] His movement was the largest mass Black movement in the history of the United States.

Repatriation in the early twentieth century addressed several needs of Blacks: a response to widespread lynching in both the North and South and widespread economic uncertainty. The Garvey Movement provided a clear articulation of the need for self-determination within a national context. Not only would the return to Africa be a means to escape the hardships of America, but it would also lead to the redemption of Africa. He envisioned 400 million Black people from around the world uniting in a common effort to rid Africa of European control and exploitation.

As in the nineteenth century when John Brown Russwurm, the foremost Black nationalist elite, encountered considerable opposition to his repatriation plans, Garvey also received sustained opposition from the Black petite bourgeoisie of his era.[18] Garvey and Garveyism was opposed by both Black labor leaders and Black entrepreneurs, such as A. Philip Randolph and Chandler Owen, editors of *Messenger* magazine, and Robert S. Abbott, editor and publisher of *The Chicago Defender.*

INDIVIDUAL REPATRIATION EFFORTS

The deportation of Marcus Garvey to Jamaica in 1927 did not signal the demise of individual repatriation efforts in the twentieth century.[19] Rather, an increased number of individual Blacks decided to repatriate. Between 1971 and 1999, several interviews were held of men and women in Africa (East and West) who had left the United States. This steady stream of people out of America and back to Africa consisted of a group of individuals whose lives and motivations have been rarely explored by scholars. Many left out of frustration over the racial situation in America; others departed because they believed genuinely that Africa was their home and that of Black people the world over. Most of these individuals had obtained middle-class status in America, yet still felt unhappy with life there. Some had comfortable teaching jobs in integrated neighborhoods, but grew tired of the "racial hassles" on the job.

Some of these repatriates were young. An eighteen-year-old girl with broad international experience decided to attend medical school in Kenya and eventually settled there. She was impressed by the harmony between the land and the people. The people lived close to the land, but used and preserved it for future generations. She valued the friendliness of the people and how she was always greeted with "Jambo" Swahili for "hello" by total strangers as she walked down the streets.

Some individuals came as spouses of Africans, and found that they had dual roles to play in adjusting to African society. For example, Clara Edwin discovered that she interacted with people in the countryside very differently than she did with European expatriates in the city. Coming from the

United States and having to live with Whites on a daily basis helped this individual to cope with Europeans.

Others enjoyed the fact that in Africa they were in the majority. They blended in with the humanity that surrounded them. One man stated unequivocally that he missed none of the "falsehood" of America. Another felt that it was his time to go, and another grew tired of working in an office for someone else. However, most acknowledged, after living in Africa for some time, that the most satisfying aspect of the new experience was the warmth and kindness of the African people. Among the African people, one repatriate found respect between men and women, adults and children. He was also impressed by the communalistic nature of traditional society, how everyone in the village worked together.

These interviews are a part of a historical continuum. The movement of African-Americans back to Africa has never ended. In the nineteenth century, the efforts were aided by Whites who perceived resettlement as serving their own political and economic ends. Through its many auxiliary branches throughout the United States, The American Colonization Society developed a rationale for resettlement (removal) of Black people from America, which enlisted the support of virtually every section of the country. There were people of various political persuasions who did not agree on the ultimate results of resettlement, yet overwhelmingly endorsed the scheme. Some believed that the colonization of Africans would help end the slave trade, and some believed that it would arrest the rapid increase in the population of Blacks in America. The northern industrialist, on the other hand, believed that the colonization of the west coast of Africa would facilitate its commercial development. However, the underlying basis of all these different views was the assumption of the innate inferiority of Blacks and the need to separate them from the rest of the American population. Despite the humanitarian rhetoric of the American Colonization Society, a society which was founded by southern plantation owners, the main goal of the scheme was to protect the property rights of the plantation owners by removing free Blacks who were considered an economic and political liability.

By comparison, in the twentieth century Blacks completely controlled repatriation efforts. Through Black institutions, such as the African Methodist Episcopal Church and the Universal Negro Improvement Association, they were able to develop philosophical justifications for repatriation, which recognized the inability of Blacks to be fully integrated into American society. These interviews are a continuing testimonial to the courage of African-Americans and their determination to discover African roots.

NOTES

1. Sheldon H. Harris, *Paul Cuffe: Black America and the African Return* (New York: Simon and Schuster, 1972), 15.

2. Ibid., 192.

3. Eli Ginzberg and Alfred S. Eichner, *The Troublesome Presence* (New York: A Mentor Book, 1964), 15.

4. Ibid., 15.

5. Robert I. Rotberg, *A Political History of Tropical Africa* (New York: Harcourt, Brace and World, 1965), 210.

6. National Archives of Jamaica, "Register of Baptisms, Parish of Portland," 1799, 1–35.

7. Robert Johnson Jr., *Returning Home: A Century of African-American Repatriation* (unpublished), 168, Archives of Bowdoin College, Brunswick, Maine.

8. Amy Jacques Garvey, *The Philosophy and Opinions of Marcus Garvey*, Vols. I and II (New York: Atheneum Press, 1970).

9. Edwin S. Redley, *Black Exodus: Black Nationalist and Back to Africa Movements, 1890–1910* (New Haven: Yale University Press, 1969), 292.

10. Crummell was born a free Black in New York City (1819), graduated from Cambridge University in England (1853), and was ordained an Episcopal minister. He lived in Liberia for twenty years, returning to America in 1873.

11. Stephen Ward Angell, *Bishop Henry McNeal Turner and African-American Religion in the South* (Knoxville: University of Tennessee Press, 1992), 154.

12. John Hope Franklin, *From Slavery to Freedom: A History of Negro Americans*, 3rd Edition (New York: Alfred A. Knopf, 1967), 439.

13. Ibid., 474.

14. Redley, 251.

15. Sarah McGill was the daughter of Dr. George McGill, one of the earliest repatriates to Liberia. She married John Brown Russwurm in 1833, mastered the Kru dialect, and served as intermediary between the Russwurm government and the Kru people.

16. Tony Martin, *Race First* (Dover, Mass: Majority Press, 1976), 6.

17. Ibid., 15.

18. John Brown Russwurm was one of the first Black college graduates in America, graduating from Bowdoin in 1826. He established the first Black newspaper, *Freedom's Journal*, with the assistance of Samuel Cornish. When he decided to repatriate in 1829, he received scorn from Black leadership, most notably from James Forten and Bishop Richard Allen.

19. Garvey was convicted in 1923 of one count of using the U.S. mail to defraud investors. It is widely believed that the charges were brought against him by the U.S. government because he posed a threat to American racism and European imperialism.

Meeting of African and African-American Students, Nairobi, Kenya, August 10, 1971

On August 10, 1971, approximately twenty African-Americans and twenty African students met to discuss the "problems" that existed between the two groups. The meeting was called together by Ronald Black, a student from the University of California at Los Angeles. The African students were from the University of Nairobi and the Americans were from the following institutions: American International University, Antioch College, Bowdoin College, Friends World College, Harvard College, Harvard Graduate School, Harvard Law School, Northeastern University, and University of California at Los Angeles.

Ron: There is a lot of criticism on the part of the Afro-Americans who come here and see that this is very much the same kind of political and economic thing we face in the United States. To some it's a disappointment. I think to most it's a disappointment because we hold a certain amount of hope that there's at least one place in the world that is headed in the right direction. That is in control of, or at least operated by Black people. But hopefully we think that there is some place in the world that is free from this sort of economic oppression. Many of us are disappointed and think that there should be things being done here, and I imagine that by the same token many of the Africans think that there are things to be done in Afro-America. Or maybe we should turn this discussion around to try and say what kinds of things we'd like to see happen in the world and possibly how to go about getting it done. Now imagine that everyone here has a general idea of what they think they would like to see in the world, but I just wonder if everyone here has an idea of how to go about doing that.

S.A.: I think that the problem is international. I think that the experience of the Afro-American can throw some light on ourselves here in Africa. . . . They can advise Africans on how the man operates.

Ron: I think that we might have to look at it as different from just seeing Africans in control of things because control is one thing but where are we going? What direction are you taking? And that one thing is kind of disappointing because it seems that the direction being taken will lead to the same sort of situation that we have now and have had in the past. It's just that Black people control and oppress other Black people. I think that maybe we should come out of the joy of seeing a Black postman and seeing a Black government and ask ourselves, now that we have a government, what is it doing for the masses of the people? Is it really an open government? I see that it really isn't that open. And I see that for the most part the same economic situation prevails here as prevails throughout the world.

George: A more interesting kind of discussion is that we have to discuss the kind of Black-White relationship, the exploitation and the historical side of colonial development, and the end of colonialism and neo-colonialism. I think that history, as an end in itself, is not interesting. History is interesting if you look at it from the dialectical materialistic approach. It will help you to explain certain phenomena and right now the problem I think that we have. That will be more of an interesting topic: the lack of communication. The absence of communication between the oppressed in Africa and in America or Europe. I think that would be a more interesting point. I think that we shouldn't look at it from Black, White, or blue, but from the exploiter and the exploited. And the most discouraging thing is like you find two people who have been oppressed and who have been exploited, but from different environments, and these people have a lot in common. They just have to unite and fight and achieve whatever they want to achieve, but because of the lack of means of communication, they just don't see eye to eye and they end up on the opposite sides of the scale. Why I brought up this point is that, like as a local person, I have come across a number of oppressed people from America, and, fortunately, however hard I have tried to create a means of communication or to learn what's going on elsewhere, the argument always ends on a personal level. So I would like to know what is wrong with them. That's my personal point of view but anyone can speak.

Ali: We should discuss the lack of communication. Why do Afro-Americans when they come to Africa—why do they have misunderstanding? Why do they have lack of communication? With the Africans? I will challenge anyone who says there is no lack of communication. There is no misunderstanding. Everything is beautiful.

George: It is a beautiful thing to call yourself an Afro-American, but it is another thing to satisfy yourself that you can be really an Afro-American unless you behave like an African.

Ron: If we should behave like an African we should call ourselves an African and not an Afro-American.

George: These are just terms of references. Like some people say there are no Americans here. But the way it looks like, culturally, there is some American culture in you. So we have to admit these things and from there go on to a different level of understanding.

Ron: That isn't what the term Afro-American means. It means that you are an African people that resides in the United States of America as a subculture in a greater culture.

Ali: How did you get that word Afro-American?

Bobby: We got tired of being called Negro. It came from people trying to . . . they use the analogy that you have German Americans, Italian Americans . . .

Ali: I'll give you my view on how this word came about. When Malcolm X was on his international tour, when he changed a lot of his views after going to Mecca and then after traveling around Africa and meeting all the African leaders, when he went to Ghana and he was addressing a meeting and he said that the Africans should never forget his Negro brother in America, an African said: "Excuse me brother we don't like the word Negro here. Can you call yourself at least Afro-American? It is more dignified." Malcolm X went back to America and took that word back with him.

Ron: I think that word was there before Malcolm X was born. It's the kind of thing. Like I think it was Du Bois earlier who had referred to Black people in America as Afro-Americans and that was . . .

John: Garvey during the twenties referred to Black Americans as Africans, or Afro-Americans. Even before that Martin Delany about 1860 used the word. He was the first one to coin the phrase "Africa for the Africans." He was a Black man.

George: I think that the problem is the crisis of identity, in that when you call yourself an Afro-American actually what I get is that you want to impress me or convince me to call you an Afro-American. You should stop worrying about what others think of what you are.

Ron: George, are there any names that you could be called that would upset you?

George: A lot of things.

Cenine: What do you call yourself?

George: George.

Cenine: That's your name. Now didn't you introduce yourself as a native of here?

George: No, I said I'm a local person.

Cenine: Yes, but what do you call yourself? What do you call yourself? As being part of what country?

George: I am a local person.

Cenine: No man, You know what I'm asking you.

George: You mean my nationality?

Cenine: Right.

George: I don't have a national identity.

Cenine: Oh, you don't?

Lydia: If you lived in America and someone called you a Negro, would you accept that? Do you think of yourself as a Negro?

George: I'm not a Negro.

Lydia: Why aren't you a Negro?

George: No, that's someone else's concept.

Lydia: That's all we are saying. That's someone else's concept of who we are. We came from Africa. We just happen to reside in America.

George: The argument is like . . . Like last week I read a *Time* magazine and this guy Roy Wilkins went to the press on his seventieth birthday and these guys asked him: "Would you like to be called Black?" He said: "No. No. I would rather prefer to be called Negro."

Ted: First of all man, in the United States there was an era when all Black leaders were White appointed. You see what I mean? They set up our leaders and said these are the folks who spoke for us. Which was a lie. So Roy Wilkins don't speak for me.

Ali: I came to know because a brother who was in this program who had left earlier on. I especially asked him to write me the names of the brothers who were coming here so that we can pay special attention to them. We'll try to take them home. That was the initiative taken on our part. That is the reason why we took part in the whole thing, and then we were abandoned. We were pushed into the Whites by the Black Americans.

John: Why were you abandoned? That's the question. Now let's have some Black American's response.

Donetta: It is a drag to have around. You know, I work with them and go to school with them, but we don't party with them. We don't hang with them. So why should we come over here and start partying with the same suckers we're trying to leave behind? I don't run with White people. I don't associate with them. They don't associate with us in the States. That's how he is.

George: But you have his money.

Donetta: That don't have a thing to do with his money. Spending his money and tipping around Mombasa with a group of crackers ain't the same thing. You know that. Going to Masai village with ten crackers to look at the Masai and pull out their little beads. Oh look what you have here! And have the Masai grab their long blond hair, you know. And have an African tell this White girl that means he likes you. No, that's what we was leaving, you understand. We don't run with White people. I don't go to no set and have no three White people behind me in the stands. So why should we come over here and do it?

George: No, no, that's no answer.

Cenine: Just answer the question. You say why is it that we do what with their money?

George: She gets into the program that was financed by a White man. She should have stayed in the United States, and not been in the program in the first place.

Cenine: Wait, wait, wait a minute! You say that it's the White man's money that brought us over here right? Did it ever occur to you that . . .

George: I did not say you. I said her.

Cenine: Wait a minute, I was brought here by White people's money! OK!

George: That's what I said, all. . .

Cenine: All right baby! Shut up and listen! The reason we were taken there in the first place was to build their country right? You think it's their money? It's our fucking sweat. Hey. So we can understand who we really are. You understand that. And from that we can fight what we think is really oppressing us baby! So I'm willing to take his money and anything else he's got to give in order to fuck him up.

Ted: Yeah look, first, of all, I think we're going around in circles. We're not accomplishing anything. First of all we have to have one person speak at a time. That's the first damn thing. The second thing is that you got to get the emotionalism out because we got too big an enemy to be dealing in emotionalism, when we supposed to be getting the shit together. Understand what I'm talking about. Let's quit talking bullshit. Let's get off your attitude. Let's get something constructive going!

George: We have something.

Ted: You sitting there, playing on a stage man. You being emotional and we can't deal with it.

George: You being emotional too. Be emotional baby.

Ken: In terms of that I think it goes back. There are several points that have to be taken into consideration in terms of Afro-Americans being assimilated by others. Number one I think it depends on the individual Afro-American you're dealing with and what his level of political consciousness is and why he's here in the first place. You know. Because I know that back in July and August there was a group of ninety niggers from the States over here by the graces of CORE. And I think it was the most fucked up group of Black people who could have come to Africa on a whole. Because as this brother said, most of the brothers in the group, who was here, was just cock hounds. They were running around trying to see how many African sisters they can fuck. They weren't here for any political reasons or cultural reasons or whatever.

Diane: But do you think there's any difference between those of us here now?

Ken: I would hope so.

Diane: There is a difference between what is and what you hope.

Ken: Well that's still an individual situation, you know.

Diane: OK. The point I'm trying to get through is that Black Americans who come to Africa have not been screened, and they have come for whatever various reasons that other people come. There are a whole lot of us. We're all different. And they're going to be different too. We can make generalities of those particular Black Americans we meet, those particular Africans we meet, those particular Europeans we meet. So that true personality and personal attitudes come into favor, but you know that's not the problem we're trying to deal with now.

Ken: I think that what she just said is a very serious thing—because not only is it that Blacks who have been here, who have created a certain picture of what Black Americans and Afro-Americans are like. It's also through the graces of the U.S. government and propaganda vehicles as well who have created a certain image in terms of what Afro-Americans are like and what they want. And it's been done to Afro-Americans in the States in terms of what their general views and opinions of what Africans are like. And the point I wanted to make is that you have to take into consideration these various facts. And to prevent the kinds of generalizations that we have. I think that, as the whole, most of the Afro-Americans who have come here have been nonrepresentative of what most Black people are like because most that come here are in government programs. They gonna reflect what the government wants them to reflect because in my travels around Africa most of the Afro-Americans I run into are working for USIS or AID or something like that. They are helping to perpetuate U.S. capitalism and U.S. imperialism in various African countries.

S.A.: I think that what divides the African from the Afro-American is four hundred years of history. This is a long time, but in the history of mankind it's a short time indeed. And we have learned from other races. The Jews have managed to get together now. They managed to get a state of Israel in 1948, and it took them about two thousand years and we have a common heritage. What we have to do now is to try to look into what we have in common because it's still on the surface. And what we have to do now is really look at ourselves and see where we have things in common because not only do we have something in common culturally, we have something in common in terms of economics. Africa is part of an international system, capitalism. And we are oppressed. We are exploited by the capitalist, and since the Black Americans are inside the structure they can be able to overthrow the system. Then we help to overthrow it on this side so that economically we can come up, Africa. Because unless Africa is cut off from this capitalist system, it will not develop. As long as it is a part of it, it will be underdeveloped.

Ali: Look at the example of Liberia where the Black Americans are looking down on Africans. And another thing the brothers missed was that the Jewish people go to settle there in Israel. They do not go back to America. The Afro-American brothers come here, stay three months or six months or one year or two years then they go away.

John: Are you interested in knowing why?

Ali: The White is of course very important. They are our visitors, but the Afro-American, mostly we come in contact with a lot of them. This congregation of Afro-Americans doesn't represent all the Afro-Americans in Africa, because like Diane said. I agree with her, most of time they come by the U.S. government. They represent America and we don't like America. And these Americans they come to me and tell me that I'm a brother. Somebody working for Institute of International Education or AID, and I go to him for a scholarship or something like that. He's an American and I'm an African. I look at him as that. He doesn't come here as the Jews do to Israel and settle and become part of Israel. I dream of the day when brothers will come over here and help us fight in Mozambique. The brothers with technical know-how, who know just as these pigs in America who are helping Portugal fight us. When the Black brothers come from Vietnam and have the knowledge and come and fight with us. Those will be brothers man. They'll be here. They'll be fighting for us. We'll be side to side. There will be no difference. We'll be brothers. I look forward to that day. I dream of it. But right now.

S.A.: We are trying to look at a problem and solve it so that our children can live a better life. This thing can be stopped. This exploitation. This degradation.

Mohammed: From my experience I have found that as an African I have many problems, and it's very hard for me to kind give my time to another brother who comes, who comes from eight thousand miles away. Like for instance, the brothers come here, they look at Africa, and they get disappointed, and go back home. If they see me with a White person walking around, they say that's a White-loving nigger, "quarharry." They never talk to me. They don't find out why. I don't have the time to go to him and say: "Why don't you come speak to me?" This is my own personal experience. It's an experience that is shared by many other Africans too. It seems to me that the Afro-Americans don't give in enough to the Africans to find out, get down a little. Give in your time and find out and share whatever problems exist.

Ali: Come to our houses.

Mohammed: Because unless you do that and kind of evoke some sense of brotherhood to me or some kind of feeling, how can you be my brother? I'm human too, you know. I would like to give my time when somebody cares for me. That, of course, is part of my human nature. I don't think that brothers pay any attention to me, that's all.

Ken: I think it's a two-way street. I'd like to respond to the comments he made. Like I'm here for twelve months and come July I'll be gone. And you won't see me for a while as well. But that's not because when I come here I say well Africa sucks, this kind of thing. The point is, in terms of our struggle, in terms of what Afro-Americans want to do, there are Afro-Americans in Africa permanently who are making a contribution. They may not be here in Kenya, but they are in Tanzania, they're in Guinea Bissau. They are in countries like that as well as when an Afro-American comes here, he's caught up between two different worlds. He's in Africa. He realizes that this is his home. This is his place of origin. And what he has to decide is where will he be most effective in trying to rid the world of this plague which oppresses all Black people. Can I be more effective here in Africa where I know there is a struggle going on and there's a need for the struggle to intensify? Or do I go back to the States? Where that's the belly of the whale of imperialism. Will I be more effective there where 30 million Black people who have lived for four hundred years and know this man excellently and know how to get to him or not? This is why most Afro-Americans who come here, go back.

Ali: We in Africa, the ones who are liberated, we say "right on" to brothers. And "fight on" in America because we know there is the main problem. If America is crushed, we automatically will be free. Because then we can fight on. At the same time we are fighting on and hoping the brothers there will be fighting on also. But if the brothers there are only fighting on to get their Black identity and stop, then, that is reactionary because we have to fight on. You have to crush the whole system because we don't want you there to fight on and join, get equality with Whites, and then continue to exploit us. We want you to fight on right up to the economic system. You crush the imperial state and try to put some sense into them. We want Black people to fight on there until they get the attitude to change the whole system.

Because if you get assimilated, you get better off there. The Whites get assimilated with you. Man, all of you together will continue to fight us. You are going to exploit us. What I'm saying is that when you go back, you should fight on, fight the whole system. That's why I say fight on to brother Eldridge Cleaver.

Dennis: A friend of mine was here, and he said that he learns about Africa through the different media. They have heard about Africa and about us in America. I think I would like to ask exactly what specific things or what impressions.

Ken: You find that most Black people in the United States don't identify with Africa, or they don't want to identify with Africa because of the way we been educated in schools. Because the media in the United States, TV, things like Tarzan movies, this kind of thing. What the U.S. government tells them. What they hear in institutions that they frequent.

George: One school is talking about cultural alienation, and another is talking about economic exploitation. And I think personally the most important thing, the basic thing, is economic exploitation. Because the origins of social inequality, whether you look at the agrarian society, industrial society, or just this society, the social inequality starts from economic exploitation. When a few people or one person tries to accumulate more than the others. So I think what we should talk about, and the basic starting issue in this continent, Africa, or elsewhere is exploitation. And that even here the people of the same culture are being used by the exploiters, the bourgeois, the capitalists to exploit people in the same cultural aspect.

Ron: You say that the main cause is economic, then you say that we're being exploited culturally.

George: No, what I'm saying. . .

Ron: Wait, wait! That is what you are saying and I've proved that the two are bound up. Now the fact that I called you brother doesn't mean that I have to join with you and we're gonna work together on the economic. Now if you think that the problem is economic, and I think it is cultural, it's all oppression and we're all gonna work on, then we're all gonna solve it.

George: Right here. The president of this nation talks a lot of what you call culture and women dancing at his home every weekend with dress up and this and that. Yet these are the same people who are being exploited. The important thing is that although they have the same culture, economic exploitation has nothing to do with culture. The cultural thing comes later on.

Sam: To me what is wrong is that the Black Americans . . .

George: Why do you keep saying Black Americans?

Sam: He has got the idea that the White man is superior and since he thinks that he is an equal. When he comes here he suffers from a superiority complex and as such he looks down at us. This is so basically.

Ken: In reference to that I think we are dealing with political and cultural consciousness. Because in the past the type of Black man who has come to Africa has not been the average brother off the street in the States. You know most Blacks in the past who came to Africa were either supported by the government, and were representatives of, say, the Black middle-class in the United States, and of course aspiring to be like White people. And in aspiring to be like White people, when they came here they're gonna look down upon you. I think that this is what has to be understood in terms of the kinds of attitudes Black Americans bring with them when they come to Africa and what this Black American's background is, because by no means is he representative of all Black people.

Sam: And this is Black Africa. When he looks at you, he looks down at you. If this complex is gonna be among you, it will be very hard for you to assimilate among us.

Ron: The only thing I can say is that if you find somebody like that, deal with him the same way you would a White man.

Ali: I don't understand why when the White Americans come to Africa they are more easily assimilated by the Africans than the Black Americans.

Cenine: How do the Whites assimilate with you?

Mohammed: They learn the language.

Ali: Let me speak my common man's language. Why is it that when the Wazungu comes to Kenya, although they have exploited us, although we are still suffering from bitterness of their exploitation, why is it that when they come here—the people, the masses of them—they easily mix with them? They talk with them. I see a lot of Whites having it good with the Africans while the Black Americans only hang around together in their own groups?

COMMENTS

The issues raised by these students in 1971 are still important today. Essentially, the question is one of identity, a problem that has faced

African-Americans from the first day of their arrival in America. When the African-American returns to the African continent, the problem becomes even more pronounced, as the African-American is confronted, not only with a romanticized vision of the African past, but also with the disturbing realities of slavery and colonialism. It is clear from the comments of these students that the transition back to Africa will not be an easy one.

2

African-American Women Who Returned to Africa

Women did not leave the United States for the same reasons as men. Neither did they decide to travel to Africa for the same reasons. While many believed that life in the United States had become unbearable, they felt that an escape for a substantial period of time would help them to reassess the Black struggle.

PAULETTE COLEN
NOVEMBER 26, 1971

Where were you born in the States?
  I was born in Thomasville, Georgia.

How long were you there?
  Oh, about four years.

And then where did you move?
  Miami, Florida.

How long where you there?
  About five years.

Did you like it?
  Miami? Yes.

And then from there you went to?
  Chicago.

And that's where you were before you came here?
Yes.

Where were you educated and what grade level did you complete?
Well I went to primary school in Miami and I went to high school in Chicago. I graduated from high school in Miami. Then I went to school in Tennessee.

Which school did you go to in Tennessee?
Knoxville College. And then I went to graduate school in Chicago.

Which one?
Roosevelt.

In what field?
I received a bachelor's in psychology and a master's in education.

When did you develop an interest in Africa?
When I was about fourteen.

What led to it?
Well I had an uncle who was working at a bus station, Greyhound bus station, and he met some Africans there one day and he brought them home. From West Africa. And they told me all about Africa, and I first thought oh that's the place I want to be. That's the place my ancestors had come from, and I figured that was my home. So I read up as much as I could about Africa and of course you know there wasn't much that you could read, but every African I would meet I would find out a lot from them. And when I got to college that's when the Black movement started in the States. And of course we had African teachers at our college and because Knoxville College was right around from the University of Tennessee. I met a lot of students from Africa then. I just learned about Africa through that way.

So you are saying you had a lot of teachers at Knoxville College?
We had about five.

How large is Knoxville College?
Well right now they have about sixteen hundred students. When I was going there they had about twelve hundred.

How old are you and are you married and have children?
I'm twenty-five. I'm married and I'm not married. I have no children.

Could you explain that again about your marriage?
I have a legal separation, and from what I gather I would have to wait three years to get a divorce here.

So you are a Kenyan citizen at this point?
No. I am not. I'm an American. But I think I'll apply for Kenyan citizenship.

You don't automatically get Kenyan citizenship when you marry a Kenyan?
No, but it's easier for you to get it if you are married to a Kenyan.

So you don't think you will go back with your husband?
No, and I don't think that I will go back to the States either.

So, you will definitely take out citizenship here?
Yes.

Have you met many other Black Americans who have decided to live in Africa?
I just met a few. I have heard of many people who are here who have settled down, most of those people are married to Kenyans.

By being in Africa what do you miss most about America?
My relatives. That's all.

You don't miss soul music and parties?
Oh, yes in a way. But those things are not that important. If I want to have soul music, I can have it here. Anything else I can have here, but relatives and nieces and nephews, people like that. I think those are the people I miss most of all.

Do you plan on going to the United States to visit relatives or will you bring them here?
I would rather for them to come over here. Like if I could save enough money I would have a couple of relatives come over. But as far as just visiting over there, I'm not too excited about that idea.

Why is that?
I've heard of people going back to the States to visit, and they are sort of disenchanted altogether. You know being away you can say, uh, I wish this or I wish that about the States. When you go back over, you see the conditions are even worse than when you left.

So you don't want to be confronted by those conditions?
Not necessarily. If I would go, I think it would just confuse me.

Has your conception of America changed as a result of being in Africa?
No.

What do you like best about being in Africa?
The weather.

What do you do for a living here?
I'm a counselor at the International Institute of Education.

Is that an American-based organization?
Yes, but they hire on local terms.

And how is it financed?
Through the New York branch.

Is it by private contributions?
Yes, basically.

What is the function of your organization?
Well, we advise students as far as what types of colleges they should go to, to specialize in different types of study. And we tell them about the American way of life, living arrangements, and what type of educational systems they have there. And help them to get scholarships in the States. And help them to make their living arrangements and accommodations and things like that. We also help them in getting visas. All sorts of problems that students would have in a foreign land.

Do you plan on working here for a while?
Yes, I plan to be here for a long time.

Why did you choose to work in an American-based organization?
One thing when I started looking for a job, I started looking with the American companies. I figured that I wouldn't have as much trouble finding a job with an American company as I would with a Kenyan company. So I found a job.

Do you find that you have been accepted as a returned sister?
With some people. And some people they ask me what am I doing here. Why aren't you in America? They think that America is just full of money and all sorts of goodies. And they want to get to America, the Africans here. And it seems that the Americans want to get to Africa. I noticed in the rural areas many people were sort of shocked to see a Black American here. They thought that all Americans were White. And they asked me how did you get there? Is your father European? So I had to explain to them about the slavery. But I noticed in the cities, more people are educated so they know a little bit about Negroes from the States.

How long have you been in Africa?
Two years.

You mentioned something about working in the rural areas. What were you doing?
I was teaching at a teachers college. I was teaching education courses and English as a second language. How to teach children English as a second language and new primary approaches. As teaching children from early school age English instead of waiting until they are in standard four and then teaching it.

You mentioned something about how you really liked the rural area. Could you elaborate on that more?
The people are more real. They are more concerned about life itself, instead of about luxuries and things like that. Their basic daily task is getting food for themselves to eat. And they just seem to be more real and more natural people. They are concerned about small things that the people in the city are not concerned about. I notice that even in Nairobi people are more phony.

That's a point that another person I interviewed made too.
Even then we started talking about the Afro-Americans in the States and whether they are real or phony. You notice that people in the South, in the rural area, they aren't as phony as the city people. And in the city, like in the North, they are just plastic.

Do you find that coming from America is an advantage or a disadvantage in terms of how you are accepted by the people?
Really I think it's an advantage because they are more fascinated by you, and they want to know all about American life. And they are eager to teach you. I know in the rural areas I learned the tribal languages, and I learned a lot about the food. People took time out to show me different things. And I learned how to plant and harvest and dig and make fire and all those things within a few months.

Made you feel as if you were back down South?
Yes.

Do you really miss the South?
Nowadays I don't because I visited the South before I left the States and I notice there had been a lot of changes. But here I really miss the rural area. It's more quiet and the people don't worry about time and you feel freer with

those people. But in the city, everybody is trying to be so European and westernized. And more so in the States.

Do you plan on going back to the States, or will you try to become a citizen here?

I plan to become a citizen here. I will never go back to the States to live. I mean I don't think that I will. I just plan to settle down in Kenya.

So do you speak any African languages?

Oh I speak tribal languages. I can speak Luo and Luola. I speak a little Swahili because the place where I was last year and part of this year very few of the people speak Swahili. You only find people speaking Swahili in the city and on the coast. So I didn't have the opportunity to learn Swahili as much as I should have.

Do you consider yourself a religious person, a political person, or an artistic person?

I don't categorize myself. I'm definitely not religious, and since I'm in Africa, I'm not political. I was political in the States but here I don't find any need to be.

Could you elaborate on that?

It's quite obvious why you have to be political in the States, but I don't quite understand why you have to be political here. There's nothing to be political about. As you know, in Kenya there is only one party, and if I, an American citizen, speak out against the party, naturally I would be deported.

So it's expedient to remain cool?

As long as the government is run by Black people, that's all right with me.

One person I was talking to was real happy coming to Africa and seeing Blacks in all kinds of positions in banks, Black policemen and the whole thing. To him that was the most rewarding thing about Africa. Then, on the other hand, you will hear someone else say that's irrelevant because the economic control is by foreigners. Would you take either side?

One thing for sure, I like the idea of having Black policemen. I won't have to be confronted by a White policeman who curses me out just because I'm Black. So that's one good thing. Now as far as having Blacks in banks and Blacks as heads and director of this and that, it's all right.

It's certainly, I think, a healthier environment to raise children in.

Definitely so. That's true.

This is the big question: Why did you leave the United States?

I left America for several reasons. I was frustrated with the racial situation there. I wanted to get out. I wanted to travel a little. And I also wanted to see what life would be like on the other side of the world. I always wanted to come to Africa because I felt that Africa is my home. And after I got here I realized that this is my home. This is the home of all Black people all over the world. So I think basically the reason was because of the racial situation. Of course, I could have escaped it by living with the middle class in the States, but deep down in, I don't think I would have ever escaped it. The only way I could escape it was to leave the States altogether.

You mentioned that you were frustrated by the racial situation? What do you mean? Weren't you very active in the community?

Of course, most people are. I was teaching in a ghetto school. I was living in an integrated neighborhood. In the neighborhood where I was living I was never confronted with racial tension and all that. But in the schools, everyday I was confronted with that, eight hours a day. And I felt there was nothing I could do. I could teach. I could work in the community and the ghetto and all that, but never did I feel that I was doing enough. And it was really frustrating to me, because if I tried to do enough I would be black-balled. I figured somebody could take my position and continue teaching, and continue working on community projects. But as far as my own peace of mind was concerned, I had to get out.

Before you left did you talk to any of your friends who had worked with you in the movement? And did they try to encourage you or discourage you?

Some tried to encourage me. Some tried to discourage me. Some said that I was running away from the problem. Some said you are lucky to get out. But I think it was about half and half.

You say you are more happy now?

Yes, I'm at peace.

In the States you hear some Black political leaders say that Black Americans can progress if we get enough people into the political system. Do you share that belief?

I don't think that at any time in the future history of America will Black people ever be free, totally free. I think they would have to be separated from the White people. Because I have strong beliefs about White people. It's just a natural instinct for them to hate Black people, and to prevent Black people from making any kind of progress. Now I think the Muslims in the States are a little bit extreme, but I think that many of those people have found that as far as the economic situation is concerned, they have made a lot of progress by being separated from the White people. And by doing for themselves. But as far as Black mayors, Black congressmen, I think that helps a little and I do mean just a little. But I don't think that Black people will ever be free in the States.

Would you say the same thing about Black economic power?

They can get a little bit of money, but when you think of it, say in relationship to the amount of money White people have, they will never even get half, or be equal to them as far as money is concerned,

Do you think that Africa consciousness, on the part of Afro-Americans, is a helpful experience?

Yes, I definitely think so. I think it's a good movement even though many of the people have been misled as far as what the Africans think, the way Africans live, and the way they dress and speak. I think that this movement is quite beneficial to Black Americans because it makes them more proud of their race.

One thing that upsets revolutionaries in America is that some brothers will be decked out in African garb, yet still join corporations, etc. Do you have any comments on that?

I think it's good for the Black people themselves. A Black woman would be afraid to walk the streets with her hair natural. So even though these Black men are putting on their dashikis and going to Ford, it's all right as one step toward Black consciousness. Even though it's not a giant step, it's just a little step. So every little step helps. It leads a person in the right direction.

As you probably know there's been some debate as to whether the major problem is an economic one or a racial one. A problem of capitalism as opposed to discrimination. What is your opinion?

I think it's racial, period. You can go any place and no matter how much money a Black man has, he's still a nigger. No matter where you go. A typical situation was when I was in the States we went to downtown Chicago to see some Black performer at the London House. We were dressed in typical American clothes. They didn't have any seats. That same night we dressed in African garb, went back, speaking pig Latin: They had the best seats in the house for us. Because they thought we were Africans. So I think no matter how much money you have or where you go, you will still be considered a nigger. So it has nothing to do with money. It's your color.

How many African countries have you visited?
Let's see one, two, three, well, I've been to the East African countries.

Which one did you like the best?
Kenya.

Do you think that a substantial number of Black Americans should come to Africa to settle?
If they have something to offer Africa. I think that Africa has enough poor people, or unskilled people. But if a Black American has some type of profession to offer Africa, I think they would be welcomed, and they would find it very comfortable.

How do you think these people would be accepted by the Africans and the government?
I think as far as the professional people are concerned, they would be accepted, because Africa does not have enough professional people. As far as the government is concerned, they would appreciate them, as far as them spending their money here and all that. But the rural people would be afraid of them because they would be afraid that these people would want to take their land. And their land they have inherited from their forefathers, and they don't want to give it up. They want their children to inherit their land.

Do you feel like an African, Afro-American, or American?
I feel like an African. I think that all Black people in the States are Africans. I don't think they are Afro-Americans or Black Americans as such. If your skin is black, you are an African.

Would you say that you are making an excellent, good, fair, or poor living here?
I think I make a fair living. Of course it's not as good as I had in the States. What I make here is about one week's salary in the States, I make here in a month. But of course, the standard of living is lower, and the price of living is lower. So it comes out about the same.

Two last questions. What do you envision the future of Afro-Americans to be?
I think that eventually more will move over here. And they will either be satisfied or not. Then, they will go back to the States. The ones who are not satisfied will go back to the States and try to adjust to the life there, and they will adjust more than they did before they came here. The ones who decide to stay will try to make the best of it.

How does it feel being a Black woman in a Black country?

Well that's really a question. Being a Black woman here, first, for one thing, I find a lot of prejudice against women period. Women don't have a say so or anything. But deep down in I think that men should run a country, and I think they should have more power than women as far as what goes on in the country. But being Black and being a woman here is all right. But just as a woman I find that I'm really discriminated against. And especially against the educated woman. I find it very difficult. Many men are afraid of educated women and they think that they are dangerous. But in the States I find it is an advantage being an educated Black woman. But one thing I like here is that they will give a Black man a job before they will give it to a Black woman. In the States, they will give a Black woman a job before they would give a Black man a job. And I think it's only fair.

DANIELLA REID
NOVEMBER 16, 1971

Where were you born?

New York.

Which part of New York?

Not the city. I was born in Suffolk County, right in the suburbs.

Do you think you have a better education as a result of being in the suburbs?

I did have a completely different education than most Black Americans because most of the schools I went to were predominantly White. Like a lot of times I was the only Black child in the class.

This is going to be interesting, sort of coming from the upper crust American society but still making that very important decision. What is your name?

[Daniella Reid.]

So, what grade did you go to in the United States?

You mean what did I complete before coming over here? My second year of high school, the second year of high school. I went to a city high school. We moved to Harlem and I went to a city high school. We moved to Harlem and I went to music and art. I don't know if you know that school. It was a completely different environment, and that is one reason why I didn't want to leave for Europe because I felt closer to my people there than I ever did before.

How long did you live in Harlem?

A year, the year just before we went to Europe.

That must have really been a culture shock, to go from Harlem to Europe. What part of Europe did you go to first?
Paris.

How old are you?
Eighteen.

And you are not married? And don't have any children?
No.

Have you met many other Black Americans who have decided to live in Africa?
I've only met one teacher who is from the States, who came here. But as far as the people at home in America, I've met many people who are interested in coming, and might decide to settle, but it is uncertain.

Yeah, I noticed that you said the people at home. You referred to America as home.
Yeah, well see, I feel that since I'm only eighteen and most of my years have been there, that was home for me. But now that I've gotten used to traveling, and everything like that—the affinity with America—isn't as great. But still that's where my family is and my friends are.

What did your immediate family, grandfathers, grandmothers, aunts, and uncles say about coming to Africa to live?
You mean me particularly or my family?

You.
They thought it was a good idea.

So they didn't really have any hang-ups that most Black Americans have?
No.

So of all civil rights groups in the States, which do you think is headed in the right direction?
Well, they are all heading the same way. They all want the same thing, so there is no one I feel closer to than others. The methods are different but it's all the same purpose.

Do you remember reading Malcolm's book when he was talking about after he had gone through an international experience and he came from Mecca, his whole idea of White folk changed, and he said it was basically a human problem and not a Black problem in the United States. Do you share his beliefs?
Well, when I went abroad I found out how much America also discriminates against other White people, that is because of capitalism, but

capitalism and racism are two different things. There is racism in America and there is imperialism abroad.

Do you think that the most serious problem is race or economics?

In America, for me it's race because that is what involves me. Now if I were White it would be different, but for me it's definitely a race problem.

If you had to give an exhortation to young Black teens in the States, what would you say?

First of all, there is not much they can do unless their parents are together about coming to Africa. But I would definitely encourage a lot more people to come. I'm recruiting my friends, as it is, to come. They are just beginning to get into the system of getting a good job and working hard and getting married and the whole thing of settling, and I think their priorities should be changed and that is what I'm trying to do. Now that they are exposed more in the States to the African culture, their own culture, they will accept my ideas better than they would normally.

Do you think that if they came here there would be any problems being accepted by local people?

Definitely not. Because especially at such a level they are really interested in meeting young Black Americans, and they both have a certain affinity because they both are interested in music. Young girls interested in boys and like my youngest sister also interested in boys. So it's the same thing generally. They could have a lot closer relationship than adults could have because they meet each other on more levels than adults do. I think adults meet each other mostly on jobs. They have a few friends whereas the young people stick together more.

Do you feel like an African, American, or Afro-American?

I definitely don't feel American. I feel I'm Afro-American because it's my culture. It's different and the types of things I'm exposed to are different than Americans, and then I'm also different from a lot of Afro-Americans in that I've also had different experiences like traveling, which a lot of people haven't had. And about being African, I'm sure I have a lot of things in common with Africa, and I will have more because being young my ideas change and no system is right for me as it is now. I can't say that I'm one thing or another because I'm really not deeply set in one place.

In the long run what type of contribution do you feel yourself making to Africa?

I hope to make a very personal contribution myself. Right now I'm considering going into medicine, and I would be practicing here.

What do you envision in the future of Africa?

Well, I can't envision now. I can only hope. And I hope that there will be an improvement, and they will be more self-sufficient than they are now and much more unity. Depending on each other rather than abroad would help their economy more.

What about the future of Afro-Americans?

America is pretty dismal. I don't think things will improve greatly in America. Things are just easing slightly and then tensing up again, so it's never going to be completely the way it should be.

When you were in the States, how did you do in high school? In terms of grades?

It was a breeze in high school. It wasn't too serious. School was just a thing you had to go through.

When you think about America and think of some of your friends, young Black kids getting shot down by the police, being involved with the Panthers, and sort of putting everything on the line in the United States like what are your relations to that? You are not there.

Well, when I first moved away from home, when I moved to Europe, I felt that I should be there. I should be getting more involved. Then I realized how frantic the struggle was, that trying to release tension, trying to gain something when they didn't even have an exact method of doing it and they were being shot down unnecessarily.

When you say unnecessarily, what do you mean by that?

Well, a lot of times it could have been prevented. And a lot of time it's something that came natural that it was going to happen anyway. The Black people in America who choose to stay, especially the young people, have to get their ideas together.

You know that's fascinating to hear the whole idea of being in the country. Similar to ancient Chinese, Indian religions. They are very nature oriented. So in a sense what you may be going through is some kind of return to the way you were originally so many years ago, that people of color even of ancient times were in close communion with things of nature, and part of our problem is that we've been taken away from that and stuck in concrete ghettoes.

And being creative and artistic in any way helps develop a person, being cramped up in a ghetto you can't really think straight.

Why did you leave America?

Well, first of all, I got tired of White people, especially the people I went to school with. I couldn't deal with that anymore. It was a time when I began to feel close to my heritage. Cause it's time now that we're getting more aware, and the only way I could find that truth was to go seek it out myself. And having a mother like I have made it more possible physically and financially.

So you are saying that your mother was probably your greatest influence?

As far as moving. Yes.

Do you think that African consciousness on the part of Afro-Americans is a good thing?

Definitely yes. They should know what is going on in America. Just like the White man is distorting the ideas and the real truth to us, they've done the same thing to Africans here concerning the Afro-American, and I hope they find out more so they don't take the White people on face value.

So you are saying they have to clean up their own backyard before they come over here trying to do anything?

And I think that it shows they're not really interested in helping the African people. It's their own interest here, you know. And a lot of Africans should realize this before they depend on them as much as they do.

What do you think of Afro-Americans who get decked out in dashikis and African robes and join Charlie's system?

The African dress doesn't mean nothing if there is nothing behind it, you know. African clothes is just like style, any other Black American style, you know.

How many countries have you visited so far?

Just Kenya and Tanzania. But I want to do a lot of traveling. We want to travel in a car throughout Africa.

Do you think that a substantial number of young Black Americans should come here?

Definitely. Even if they don't come to settle, just to visit. Because it will change their whole outlook of what's happening in the world as well as in the States. And since they are the ones who are going to be moving up and becoming leaders and getting jobs, they should be more aware of their heritage and what they can do.

Do you help your mother out around the school at all?
Yes. I do some teaching, and a lot of the students consult me concerning what's going on in school.

Other than that. Do you work anywhere else?
No. I don't.

Do you find that you've been accepted as a sister who has returned?
Yes, definitely. They always say I'm African, and they want me to be completely integrated in Africa. They want me to marry an African—in fact they are sure that I will.

Do you think you will?
I don't know.

Do you plan on becoming a citizen?
Umm! I really don't know about that. I'd have to really check it out and visit more countries. I want to visit all of Africa. I know I'll never return to the States to live. Wherever my mother is that will be home. As far as what country I'll prefer, I'll have to travel more to find out.

Do you think you'll stay with your mother? I mean how long? What age? etc.
Well, that will be my main base. I can't say what age because I'm interested in traveling around. So I won't be at home much. But I'll still have a place I can call home.

Do you speak any African languages?
Well, I speak a little Swahili and I'm learning, I want to really learn Swahili and then possibly Luo which is the language of the main tribe in the area we are.

That's interesting. Do you find that many of the Luo bring up tribal problems within Tanzania and Kenya?
Well, there are some tribal barriers, but where we are isn't that great because of such a large majority of Luos.

Do you consider yourself a religious person, political person, artistic, or any other type of person?
Definitely not religious in a Christian sense and I'm still finding myself in that area. I know some people who have gotten closer to the African religions also, but I'm still checking that out. As far as politics is concerned, I'm not involved in government structure per se, but I'm involved in trying to change things.

Change things here in Africa or in the United States?
Well, both ways.

Where are you going to do the most changing eventually?
Here, where I'm at.

What about an artistic person?
Well, art was my first love. That's why I went to the High School of Music and Art. I find great subjects here in Africa for art.

Do you do any painting?
Yes, I do painting.

Do you miss soul music?
Well, we get that over here and people send me things. So I don't miss it that much.

So you are saying that you have to have some type of contact with Black America, the music and things like that.
Umm, well, the music and the people are still a part of me. They will always be a part of me I think. I still feel like dancing to soul music when I hear it. But it's nothing that I miss great enough that I'll want to go back.

What is so attractive about being here that sort of balances out?
I like being here at my age because the young people here are very much aware of Black Americans also, and I have very interesting discussions with people of my own age and I feel very close to the Africans now than I probably would have been later because now I'm still able to accept new ideas, you know. I haven't been in a tradition where I'm used to the same thing.

Have your conceptions of America changed as a result of being in Africa?
No. I knew what was going on before I came here.

The reason I asked is because some people I've run across say that now living in Africa and seeing what this place is like makes you appreciate America more.
No, definitely not. I definitely don't feel that way, The exact opposite.

What do you like best about Africa?
The beauty of the place and the people. The way they both fit in together. The natural environment, especially out where we are in Shirati where the people and the land combine together. You know it's not like they're using the land and they are separated from it. And the warmth of the people also, Before coming here I wasn't used to always greeting anybody I meet on the street but then you get so used to saying "Jambo," "Jambo" anytime you meet anybody crossing the road.

CLARA EDWIN
NOVEMBER 17, 1971

Where were you born in the States?
I was born in Coalwood, West Virginia.

How long did you live there?
I stayed there from 1944 to 1950 and in 1950 we migrated to Los Angeles.

How long did you live in Los Angeles?
Stayed there from '50 until '65, 1965.

That's when you came here?
Yes.

Where were you educated and to what grade level did you go?
I went up to two years' college.

Was that at Bluefield State?
Bluefield State, yes.

When did you develop an interest in Africa?
I think from a very young age actually. I think it started from the time I could realize that there was such a thing as geography and such a thing as environment wider than my front yard or my backyard.

And you think your family had something to do with that?
I mainly attribute that to my father, because he had always been rather nationalistic in all his views and philosophies and concepts. So I think maybe he must have gotten it from his father who died at . . . his father died when he was sixteen, but I understand that his father was very astute culturally. Black cultural affairs and trying to introduce his children to a trend of thinking that was what he would call now nationalistic thinking. So I just attribute the whole thing to my father and his teachings.

How old are you and are you married and have children?
I'm twenty-seven now. I was married in 1965 to a Masai who is from Kenya and we divorced a year later and I have not married again yet.

Do you attribute the divorce and some of the problems you encountered to the difference in culture between the two of you, or something else?
Well, unfortunately I cannot attribute it to any one thing. It was a conglomeration of things, but I think that basically it was personal. Just between the two of us. I don't think culture had very much to do with it. Of course, it had to have some fraction simply because all things evolve into

one thing. So that was mainly just between the two of us individuals, you know. I don't think it was mainly cultural. No.

Did you find that your perspective was widened as a result of being married to a Masai?
You mean widened in the sense of being in Africa . . . or. . .

Well just in that sense of encountering such a different experience. Or was he so westernized that it wasn't. . .
Oh that way, no not while I was married. In fact, I can't say that the year I was married contributed very much to anything. Most of my learning how to survive here was attributed after I left, after my husband and I separated.

Have you met many other Afro-Americans who have decided to settle in Africa?
Mainly limited to the women, Black American girls who are married to Kenyans. I have met casually couples who come for visits. You know, you met them. I used to work for an international airlines, and I would meet them that way. Also at parties and things like that. You know them for a day or two. But I do have one or two friends that I've had since 1965 when I came, and they are married to Kenyans also so we have quite a lot in common. So you sort of remain attached to them.

How are the feelings as far as their marriages go?
Well, most of them are doing very well. However, I do believe that Black American girls, for some reason, and this is simply my opinion, we have more difficulty in adjusting simply because we look like an African. I mean it's the small things, most of the time, that makes life meaningful. Now to another African, when they first see you, because you resemble them and because you are familiar to them, the first inclination is to think this person is like me. Now when you react differently from them, then of course this is why you get reactions from us and reactions from them. Now Black American girls have much more adjusting to do, say than a White American, because first of all her husband is a White European. I'm limiting to Americans because that's where I'm from so I speak in that context because that's what I know about. White American girls, because they look different from the Africans, just physically looking different, they were excused to begin with from many things which they are suppose to know and many adjustments that they are supposed to make because they are different. Now with us, we are not always excused because we are not that different. Even the husband expects you to know certain things. He doesn't expect to, but it

just evolves naturally that he assumes that you know certain things that you don't know, simply because culturally we are very, very different.

Where did you meet your husband?
In college, in Los Angeles. At the summer school when I went back in '62.

By being in Africa what do you miss most about America?
Nothing, I don't really miss anything. However the emotion that I will have and I do have is a strong sense of attachment for the beauty of the Black American culture which is completely unique. There's not another one anywhere in the world. And it was only until I was out of that perspective that I could look back and see that it is very unique. I'm just proud that was my origin. As far as missing things, of course, I'm attuned to things happening there. I keep alert with current events. And I can still feel unity and all of these emotions when the people are doing something like they are now. But I really don't miss anything there. You find life here is too full, too rewarding, and there is too much in a day that you have to do and that I find to do, that I just don't have time to miss things in America. But I can say that I've come to appreciate our culture, the Black American, because it is very wonderful and unique.

What are some of the hallmarks of the culture that you enjoy?
Well, I just can't say one specific thing because this is just an emotional outburst. In other words, I feel that because I have been here and had to adjust to a different culture. And you find that here the progress of the African is slower than I would like for it to be. And I can observe after some time that Black Americans are making greater and faster progress against greater odds. I should think that is the one hallmark that I can point, it is not a specific. But it's a general thing. But that's the element that the emotion is based on. Simply because the Black American has been completely at a disadvantage. Completely at a disadvantage, yet he has managed for whatever reasons that were there for him to do that. He has managed to progress at a faster pace and to secure even though he may not think so. If he comes here and tries to survive here, then he can recognize that he has done more in a shorter period of time with less than the African here in Africa in his homeland is doing now with more.

Has your conception of America changed as a result of your being in Africa?
Basically not.

What do you like best about Africa?

The feeling of freedom, the very thing that Africans outnumber the Europeans that are here. But I like the general feeling I have here of well-being, freedom, and security. I could just use adjectives all down the line. But I don't feel as though I'm threatened here, by anything. Any holocaust could come and I know that I'm still going to survive here. Whereas in the states you always had that feeling that everything must be in a sequence and in order for you to survive. Here I don't have that type of thing.

What do you do for a living here?

I'm in the airlines and travel work. Mainly because my mother is still in the States, and I find it necessary to go back and visit her at least once a year. And of course salary scales here are not what they would like them to be, so I found that I had to work for the airlines in order to get rebates to go back to the States. But then most people say that you stumble into something. I found that I enjoyed it, and I liked it very much so I've been in for the last five years.

What specifically do you do?

Anything pertaining to airlines. Writing tickets, making reservations, doing fares, things like that.

Do you find that you've been accepted as a returned sister?

No. Normally Africans always view you as a foreigner. Even though you may look like a Kikiyu, a Masai, a Kalenjin, or any other tribe you want to look like. Like I resemble any ordinary girl from the coast, but I don't think like one. I don't react like one. I can't because we are culturally two different people. The only thing I can do is try to assimilate. Now the African always views you, or views one as a foreigner. No matter how long you stay, you've been here twenty years and they can accept you as a friend, and as a close companion, but you are still a foreigner always until you die. I think for a woman the only way and possible for a man, the only way that they can ever be indigenous is through their children. But as far as myself or any other Black American who is married to one of them, you don't have this strong attachment of brotherness. It is not in their vocabulary like it is in the Black American vocabulary.

Do you find that coming from America is an advantage or disadvantage?

Definitely an advantage because the one thing the Americans have done is to make the United States seem like it's a great country, which actually it is. If you really look at what the country has to offer, it is. If the people could look at what they're supposed to follow as far as the Constitution and things like that, it is. It's only the social corruption that's going on that's spoiling it. But now America definitely has managed to blow her image up. And I find that because I am from America, I get into a lot of things, places, jobs, people that I would not have met say if I was from some other country, France, for instance. So because you are from America, automatically you're great.

Do you plan to go back to America to live or do you plan to become a citizen here?
I'm already a citizen. I've been a citizen since '65. I took citizenship out two months after I came.

Do you think that you will ever go back to the United States?
To live, no, but to go to some other place in Africa, I like Africa too much.

And even though you think that the United States is fairly good, you wouldn't like to go back there?
No, the only attachment I have is a feeling for my people there, for their struggle and to understand that they're struggling and to have sympathies and to be happy when they are making progress and to be sad when they are shot up and this sort of thing. But to go back even to go back to fight for the cause I have no interest in that cause because I have found a greater cause in Africa.

You were here when Malcolm X was killed in the States in '65?
But I was in the bush and it only had the effect on me, not even on my husband then.

What type of effect did the murder of Dr. Martin Luther King have on you?
On me personally? Well, every time the news came on here and they would say Dr. King, I would just expect that they were going to say that he had been assassinated or something like that. So when it came on the news I became silent inwardly, but it was not a shock because I had always expected it. Now I wasn't emotionally affected until I went to one ceremony. They had a mass in the cathedral here, and I went there and words were said and it was mainly Americans who went and American officials, ex-students from America. It wasn't a shock to me. Say for instance when Mr. Mhoua died it was a shock, and it affected me for weeks because I wasn't expecting that at all, and he was the only hope we had, you see. But with Dr. King I was already expecting it, and it was just a matter of time. And it just seemed that was the order of the day. Coming from there.

Do you speak any African languages?
Well, no, that is a very interesting thing and when you are interviewing

people I wish you could ask, to try to find out why it is that Black American
girls do not learn Swahili. I'm sure there is a psychological hang-up as to
why we don't. Now I've been here five years, and I studied Swahili a year
before I came and I was speaking very good grammatical Swahili. I
lived in the bush when I first came to Kenya and the house steward was a
Kikuyu, and Kikuyu are very proud of their dialect and they won't speak
anything but Kikuyu and they are very bad Swahili speakers. So I phased
off into Kikuyu sounds, and every time I spoke Swahili it was grammati-
cally correct so nobody understood a word I was saying badly. Now
when I say understood, they would correct me the wrong way. This sort
of thing. Now my husband, being a Masai and his living in Kikuyu and
your best friend being from (Sayshell). Whenever we were, as a group,
there was English, nothing else. If we went outside to visit as a group
there was English, nothing else. If I went outside to visit the neighborhood farmers, the wives there, it was English because they didn't speak
Swahili. It was Kikuyu and Kikuyu was spoken, so it was either Kikuyu
or English. So I stayed there a year and phased into Kikuyu sounds.
When I left there, I moved into the city in Nairobi and I was working for
the United States Information Service, and the only sounds I heard there
were English and Kamba, because the drivers and messengers that was
my little cubbyhole I was working with them. Now I stayed there for two
years, and I found that the problem was that most of my friends, immediate and very close friends, were from various tribes. My best friend could
be a Kikuyu, a Luo, a Kamba, or a Kaledji. When they are with me, they
only speak English. If there was another friend, they would speak
another dialect, but not Swahili. So I can speak Swahili, but I couldn't
hold this interview in Swahili. But they say Swahili is good for getting
around the restaurant or shop, stuff like that. I can do that but now the
interesting thing is that most of the Black American girls who are here
did not learn Swahili. And I've been to classes five different times and
stayed in them three weeks and dropped out and it's not me. There's one
other girl Kathy Mathi, who has been here twelve or thirteen years, and I
speak better Swahili than they do. We don't learn Swahili and there has to
be reasons for it. I wish somebody could probe into it. I would be very interested to know why. I think it has something to do with the acceptance
thing. For instance, when a girl comes here we joke among ourselves
that you behave as if you are suffering from a cultural shock. When you
wake up one day and realize that you are 12,000 miles from anything
familiar, your mother, father, family, and you're over here in this country with all this stuff that goes on. I mean you just say, my God, what am

I doing here? Why am I really here and do I want to go through this funny psycho thing? And once you get over that, you sort of fall into an equal norm and you manage. Now when you come here you have to accept so many things and so much from your husband's side. You have to accept him, for his family. You have to accept even in the office the procedure for typing if you're a secretary, answering the telephone. Everything you have to change from what you have been taught. You change because this is based on the British system as well, plus all the African cultural tidbits here and there. Now because she has to accept all of this and adjust to it. I think that the reason we don't learn Swahili is because we feel that the one thing that we have to keep is the English, and you just have to accept that we don't speak Swahili.

Do you consider yourself a religious, political, or an artistic person?
Political.

Political in what way?
I'm very conscious of politics here and in America.

That's interesting because the majority of the people say that they are political in the United States, but they aren't here because being an outsider, if they mention anything about the government.
Well, I think. Are these citizens?

No they're not. Most of them aren't, but have been here for five or six years.
I've never had that fear and I find that African politics is so interesting and is so unique that I say what I want to say. All they can do is to put me in jail, but they don't want to do that.

They can't deport you. Do you still have your American passport?
No, I doubt if they would deport me, they could probably send me back to the States if I accepted, but normally if you are a citizen like that, no. Say like when Carolyn Okelo Odongo went to prison, they asked her whether she wanted to be deported or go to jail? Well, I'll just be like her and go to jail if I ever become involved in politics.

Who is she?
She is an American married to a Luo, Tom Okelo Odongo.

And so what happened? I'm not familiar with the whole story.
All this was when Odinga formed a second party KPU, and Okelo Odongo was Odinas's right-hand man and Carolyn was his private secretary. So they were very much involved in politics so they arrested her. They arrested her before they did Tom. And she went to jail and stayed eighteen

months, a political prisoner. Then she came out, and about six months later they arrested Tom. The thing about Africans is that they fight and make up very quickly, so you find, say, like going to jail, people get worried that going to jail is the end of their life, but not here. Tom went to jail, J. D. Colly went to jail, all of them, but they are still holding top positions in the government because, like I say, you'll always survive here no matter what happens. You just don't feel threatened even if you sit in jail for two years.

Now this person you mentioned, is she still living here in Kenya?
Yes, you can find Tom at the extramural extension of university college at Dagoretti.

Where is that?
Dagoretti is north of here on the way to Kahete.

Why did you leave America?
To come here to get married.

And that was basically social?
Yes, I just came to get married—that is all.

Did you find you had to prepare yourself psychologically or in any other ways for coming to Africa?
I just up and came.

And once you got here, did you have to then adjust?
No, because I was also anxious to come to Africa. My father had been to Nigeria for two months, and he had planned to move to Nigeria. So Africa was just there always and in fact I had always assumed that I was going to live here. I don't know why.

From what age can you say that?
About as long as I can remember because I remember we always talked about it, it was just always there. You can take a small child and you can mold it into anything, and my father was very careful about what went into my head. Evidently he had always talked about it. I can remember, for instance, one thing when we first went to California and we lived in a trailer for Blacks and I went to a board of education. I went to that school and my mother was conscious about straightening my hair as when I was in West Virginia where she would just wash it and braid it up. But there she wanted to straighten it real straight and put ribbons on it and all. I remember one day my mother washed my hair and it was drying and it was like it is now, and my daddy came in and said, "Oh there's my little African queen." Then he said to momma, "why you keep straightening the baby's hair like

that?" So there was the thing, I remember that and he used to do things to me like that all the time—of course, I didn't know why this was happening. I was young. So I can't remember when Africa became so important. It was just always there. I think it was just him. His teaching because I remember on Sunday when we got the paper, I would sit in his lap, and he would read things to me and put his own words in them. He was indoctrinating me all the time. There was this comic strip called "Mohawk, Lion of the Jungle," and he would read that and put a lot of things in them that aren't even there, glorifying Africa. So I don't remember when it started, because it was always there.

How many African countries have you visited?

I've only been to Uganda, Kenya, and Tanzania. Simply because working for the airlines, every time I have a leave, I mean with my mother still in the States, every time I had to go to see her. Now she is planning to come over here in the next two years.

To live or to visit?

No to live. Then I get our house built because she's not well and she has to be stabilized. She can't move around and dad and I are still moving about. Now I have been all over Kenya. But because of having to go to visit my mother I haven't been able to visit other African countries. I know people in all of these places, and I want to spend some time in their homes and in the bush. I have been all over Kenya except the northern frontier. I haven't been to Dar es Salaam yet because of Swahili and the people that I know there. I can't communicate with them unless I know Swahili, but I have been down to all the border places and to Arusha, Moshi, Tanga with some friends, from Kenya. I've been to Kampala. I went to see my mother in April, and I don't want to go next year because I have a chance to go to West Africa. Nigeria, Accra, Senegal, Liberia, and Morocco. So if that comes through, I'll go and spend two months, take my leave and another month.

Do you think a substantial number of Black Americans should come to Africa and settle?

I don't think that as many should come that do come sometimes.

Why is that?

Well, I have the feeling that I might be wrong because sometimes I get rather conceited and one sided in my ideas. I feel that the concept put forth now about Africa within the Black American sphere over instills a sense of independence. That when they come, they are expecting complete independence, and they are not expecting to find the old hang-ups that are in the

United States. But you'll find that the same hang-ups are here, and you really have to have an idealistic philosophy about Africa in order to come here and sit in a gold mine and not really, in some instances, be able to partake of the gold. And because of that, a lot of Black Americans come here with this love of finding independent thinking, and free acting, and when they come, they find the complete opposite. They become so despondent that they slip back into a capitalistic type view and philosophy, and they find they have to fall back on their American culture. They are so real that you just have to have a real love for Africa, or otherwise you just can't adjust to some of the things that happen here.

Do you feel like an African, Afro-American, or an American?

I always feel like a misfit because as I said I feel, and this is strictly my feeling, that I will never be indigenous. Now, I feel associated to Africa but I do not feel indigenous because I cannot, as a woman, retrogress to be indigenous. In order to be an indigenous woman in Africa, I have to retrogress my feminine aspects because the status of women here is not what it is in America. I'm not saying either one is good over the other. I'm saying it is different, and as a female I'm a misfit because of relationships with men that I may find straining because of a cultural difference between us. An African girl would not have any difficulties in other aspects—work, politics, things like that. Again, I only think that a woman would be indigenous through her children if she has children by an African.

Even though you feel like a misfit, you would rather stay here than the United States?

Now when I say misfit I don't mean that in a negative sense. I just mean it like a missing piece out of a puzzle. Let me put it this way: It's like sitting on a fence. I shouldn't say misfit because that connotates negative thoughts. I'll just say I sort of sit on the fence and when the occasion arises I can jump off on either side, depending on what is required. Say if I go up country to a village that I have never been to, and I do quite often. I'm with some friends who are from there, and we go right into the bush, which is terrific. I love it. If I have never been there and I don't know the dialect, the first thing I do is learn the greetings. Learn how to greet the elders, good-bye, thank you, and how to say my name in that dialect which takes about five minutes. So whenever I go I can communicate, and it doesn't take a whole lot of words to do that, and the people are always grateful for a foreigner and outsider who can at least greet them in their own dialect. When, on the other hand, say in the office I have to deal with a European with a colonial mentality, I jump off and I'm an expatriate because I can jump off and be bad with him and really cut him down where an African girl couldn't do it. But yet I look African enough until they mistake me, until I cut them down. Then they say well, hell, this isn't an African because she wouldn't dare say anything like that to me. So I just sit on the fence and whatever is the order of the day, that's what I am.

Would you say that you are making an excellent, fair, good, or poor living here?
Compared to what I would be doing in the States or you mean . . .

Take it from what I said and draw your own conclusion.
Well, I'm not a materialist, never have been, so I would say that I live excellent. I don't have a television, or fabulous clothes. I wear things that are necessary, and I have a car because it is necessary and I'm happy, very happy. I'm not a materialist at all so it doesn't mean a thing. To me, I'm living real good.

What do you envision the future of the Afro-Americans to be?
Oh, well, I think they are going to be one of the greatest cultural groups in the world because they are now and they just don't know it. When you think of what they've done against the odds they had, they have done so much more than many other people who had more advantages. I think eventually they are really going to be recognized, and they are going to recognize themselves and acclaim themselves as the greatest cultural group in the world.

You don't think that they'll ever be powerful politically?
I think they can as far as observations I have now: I think they are going to be in a unified way. They are moving toward that now by becoming more unified in all of their approaches and aspects. When they get to this sphere and when they attain that, it is going to affect Africa, and I guarantee you that it will not take place in Africa before that Black cultural group had won it. Indirectly, what you do there affects what happens here. Strangely enough I believe it does, that's my opinion.

Another thing is whether you think that the major problem in the United States is an economic one, capitalism, or whether it's a problem of race discrimination? Would you take either side?
Both. I don't think you can even separate the two; both have contributed as much as the other. It's like a husband and wife when they are divorced. You say, what happened? He says, "it's her fault," and she says, "it's his fault," but they don't realize it was them. It wouldn't have happened unless there were two of them there having it happen. So I think race and econom-

ics go hand in hand. Here we have freedom with either one and both of them running hand in hand together. So we are still in neocolonialism because we don't have economic freedom, and we won't get it until the Black Americans have totally and completely economically gotten on their own which I think they will.

OK? This is a final question. What kind of exhortations can you give to Black women in America or a Black woman in Africa?
    Oh dear, in what respect?

I don't want to narrow it down. In any respect you want to give it.
    The only thing that I can think of, through reading. They should have more respect for the Black man and help him more and understand when he has hang-ups because African men have hundreds of hang-ups, and you just have to understand and accept them. It takes all of your feminine qualities not to overpower him because certain things you can see that he can't see because he has problems that are very deep and cultural. But I understand that Black women are doing this, you see. Just to say, accept him, understand him, and be his helpmate and always be conscious of the fact that you are the indoctrinator of your children. And an educated mother makes an educated child and an educated child makes an educated nation. She must realize that everyday everything she said to her child is important and not let the children get away from her without instilling within them certain basic and foundational philosophies which they are going to need as a Black child in the world. Not only in America or Africa but in the world Black people are on their way to a very big glory, and every African child or Black American child should just be aware of this, which I think I could think of as a female to another female that has to be stressed. Your greatest duty is to be a helpmate to your man and indoctrinate your children to be Black, to think Black, and really become aware of all they have to do because he just can't grow up having these pseudonorms. He has to be real and basic. We have a problem here in Africa of the people not really being aware of this. Nowadays we have women who are married to influential African men in government or business, and in an attempt to try to be civilized she is destroying many of the African cultural traits that her child needs. You meet this African child. He knows Scottish dancing, all the kings and queens of England, and yet he doesn't know who James Ngugi is or who Ocot Otik is and he can't even speak his father's dialect. Now this is the mistake that African women are making, not the majority because they are still in the bush and she is still the dominant figure. I'm speaking of the assimilated African woman who is trying to be civilized in the city, with the city life. As for the Black American woman, she should just be conscious of her role and what she had to teach her children.

I was talking to another sister, and she said that the African man feels threatened by an educated woman.

Yes, he does, because she can out think him and it's a delicate thing and funny. You see, even in the bush an African woman is dominant and she is dominating. She is the backbone of the family structure and man even. She does not dominate him. Does that make sense? But when you get an educated African woman, who has assimilated, then she is like me—a Black American who can be the backbone of the man. I can be the dominant figure in the family and I can be the work horse, but in doing all of this we do not know how not to superimpose ourselves. We don't know how not to dominate him. It's just a small thing. Every minute that you can't see it, sometimes, but that is the cause of many a Black American girl and African man breaking up. Even myself, because I was too strong for him and I could not be the mule and the driver too. I'm still trying to learn how to do this. It's a very delicate thing to do. I find that Black American girls who are not extroverted make the best wives. Now I'm an extrovert. Vernestine Mybia is an extrovert, but there is a girl here named Kathryn who is an introvert. Even if she was in the United States, she is a homebody; she sits home and bakes cakes. She doesn't even know who the vice president is now. She knew Tom Mboya because her husband was a Luo. She doesn't know what KADU or KANU is but yet she can tell you how to make Hungarian goulash or how to make African idiom and she does needlework. She is basically an introverted homebody and I don't say it negatively. But her will centers around her house and buying a new pair of shoes. When she reads the news, she reads the fashions. But won't bother with international or African news or this sort of thing. She and her husband are very happy, and they will always be and won't have any problems because she is the backbone. He doesn't make a decision without her. She still makes all the decisions in the house. But she is not dominating him. She is doing it the way an African woman should do it and that is because she is introverted. I'm an extrovert, if the home is there and needs work, I won't have the time because I'm too involved with thinking about other things. And worrying about the wars and what Angela Davis is going to do and who got shot. You see these things bother me and I have to be concerned about them, so therefore I find that I don't have the patience to not dominate which, in a way, is bad.

It seems like, from the description you are giving of African women, they are in the same position as some American women are in, particularly the White women. And that what they are rebelling against when they talk about women's liberation. The whole thing of dealing with kitchen duties and not being able to take a job as opposed to getting involved in politics.

You see there is a slight difference in that here in Africa, the duties of a woman are far greater than those of the man. For instance, she has to take care of the farm, build the house, do all the cooking, pay the school fees, find clothes for the children, take them to the hospital when they are sick. She has to see that vegetables are harvested and taken to the market, put money in the bank, and take care of the plumbing. She does everything and then that man enters the house he has nothing. Yet he dominates and rules. It is minute because in America when he walks into the house he doesn't dominate and he doesn't rule. It's hard to explain and I'm not sure that I'm getting it across. Here, African men are just downright unreasonable.

Is that from our perspective or the African woman's perspective?

No, because she is accustomed to it and has been taught this for as long as she can remember. You don't get this from the African city woman. You take an African city woman like me, where if her husband goes out with another woman, you might find her locking him out of the bedroom or going out with another man. Well, you see she can't do that because up-country if a wife goes in town carrying her potatoes on her back and she sees her husband sitting in a bar with another woman, laughing and talking, she is not going to do anything. Nothing, because he is the dominant character. But in town, like I say, when he comes home, she's locked him out the bedroom and made a fuss. This is when the husband says you are difficult in retrogressing to adjust to a lot of these cultural traits that are accepted.

One thing, the last thing is why do you feel so optimistic about the future of Black Americans? The majority of the people, as a matter of fact I think you are the first one, and I've interviewed nine people, including your father, and they say the future of Black Americans was very dim and you seem to think different.

Well, if you think when I see things here and I see what he came from and where he was then to now, I just feel that he is not going to stop. What's happening now is that he is in a revolt and like all cultural groups in a revolution this is the Black days. When you are at the bottom, there is only one way to go and that is up. So I feel that after being here and seeing what the African has—he has a gold mine and he's not even using a fraction of it. When I see what the American Blacks have, which is nothing, and yet they are managing against very great odds to even find their identity and unity. They aren't going to stop. They can't go back from where they came. They are going to go forward.

MRS. FLORA REID
NOVEMBER 1971

What part of the States are you from?
New York City.

Where were you educated and what grade level did you go to?
Oh, I was educated in New York City and the suburbs. I went as far as my bachelor's degree and a year of my master's.

And what were they in?
In sociology, my major was sociology.

And what schools were they?
City College, which is now City University. I went to Hofstra, Long Island, and Adelphi for graduate study.

When did you develop an interest in Africa?
That's difficult to say because I can't remember when I didn't have an interest in Africa. I think it probably started with my father because he had a relative who was in the Merchant Marines and when he was very young his cousin, I think my father was probably still in the south, his cousin made a trip home and said that it was his last time and to tell everyone good-bye because he was never coming back again. So I guess he was the first expatriate in the family. My father used to always tell us, "Don't believe anything you read about Africa because White people don't want you over there." So I think that was something that started very young.

So did your father become an expatriate?
No, he didn't.

Did he visit Africa?
No.

How old are you?
It's too personal.

Are you married?
No, I'm divorced.

How many children do you have?
Three.

Are they with you in Africa?
Two are with me.

Have you met a great many Black Americans who have decided to spend a great deal of time in Africa or want to become citizens?

Actually, I've only met one other.

Where was that?

At the school I'm working at.

Is he or she an expatriate now?

Yes, he wants to become a citizen of Tanzania.

By being in Africa what do you miss about America?

All of my friends and relatives and I also miss all that bread I was making. But not much.

You mentioned before that you had a job. What kind of job is it and how much do you make?

My last job in the States I was directing an antipoverty program in the suburbs of New York City, well, suburban New York.

A Black suburb or mixed?

The largest minority were Puerto Rican, and Blacks were the second largest minority which is a bit odd.

Have your conceptions of America changed as a result of being here?

My conceptions of America?

Yes, I mean do you look at America in a different light or more or less the same?

No, it hasn't changed.

What do you like best about Africa?

I have to name one thing? Oh, a lot of things. I'd say then people, the topography is fantastic and I think that's it.

What qualities do you find missing from the so-called elites in the city?

The people, I think they have a quality of humanity and mainly very simple people, so-called peasants. I think they're difficult to put into words. They're proud and very polite and formal to some extent but very, very warm.

Do you find that quality missing from the so-called elites in the city?

No, it's not missing, even the city Africans have more of it than White people.

What about as compared to Black people in the States? Do they have this humanity you're talking about?
Yes.

But not quite as much as the brothers here?
No, I wouldn't say that because I've found it a quality of Black people. I think human relationships are very important to Black people wherever I've met them. I think it is more important than among White people. I think they haven't lost a touch of relating to other people.

What do you do for a living here?
Teach.

What grade level?
First and second form, which is like the first and second year of high school.

I think you mentioned that it was in a small village in Tanzania?
Well, actually we are near a village, but not in one. About four miles away.

Would you say the school is in the country or the bush?
In the bush.

Do you find that you've been accepted as a returned sister?
Yes, to a large extent.

You haven't run across too much hostility?
None at all.

Do you find that coming from America is an advantage or disadvantage to you in terms of relating to African brothers here? When they hear that you're an American, does that sort of set them off?
Yes, I've found that it set them off, the ones that I've met. Of course, I only communicate with those who speak English and have had a certain amount of education.

Do you plan to go back to America to live, or do you plan to become a citizen here in Africa?
I plan on becoming a citizen someplace. I'm not sure where. If I don't become a citizen here, I don't plan to live in the States again.

Do you speak any African languages yet?
No.

Do you consider yourself a religious, political, or artistic person?
   An artistic person.

Artistic in what way?
   In a very practical way. I'm teaching and although my education had been in sociology, I feel that my trend is more towards teaching. It's just what I've been doing for a living. I basically feel more artistic.

Have you done anything in art?
   Yes, I've worked in craft quite a bit, and other things.

This is the big question: Why did you leave America?
   I felt a disaffinity in America, and I don't feel that there is a future for Black people in America. I don't think it's practical for them all to leave because it's next to impossible, but the more that leave the better for Africa.

Are there any particular incidents in your life that all of a sudden made you decide to come to Africa? Or had you been thinking about it for a long time?
   Before I came I had been thinking about it for a long time, seven years, which meant that seven years before I came to stay I had visited here and had decided that one day I was coming back to stay.

What part did you visit?
   All the countries? Ghana, Nigeria, Tanzania, Ethiopia, and Kenya.

One of the problems that Black people have in coming to Africa is a financial one, but you seem to have overcome that barrier. Do you think this is a real barrier? Is it possible to raise sufficient funds to at least visit Africa?
   Oh, yes, for the people who should come I don't think there is really a barrier because no one should come who hasn't some sort of background or training, education or so forth. That type of person can make quite a bit of money in the States. If you look at the way they are living in the States, usually they're spending that money on homes, cars, clothes, vacations, and things like that. So saving a few years would be sufficient if they ever wanted to leave, so for them I don't think the money would be a handicap.

Do you think that Africa consciousness on the part of Afro-Americans is a good thing?
   Yes.

Which African country have you enjoyed the most and why?
   Actually I've enjoyed Kenya the most when I visited here before because I knew more people. I knew people who could show me around and introduce me to interesting people so it made the visit better. I got to see more than an ordinary tourist or visitor usually sees. But now I feel I've enjoyed

Tanzania more because I feel I'm contributing something there. Also because of the relationship I have with the people there.

So do you think that a substantial number of Black Americans should come here to settle?
Yes.

Any particular part of Africa?
No, I think that is one of the beautiful things I like about Africa is the fact that it is so agrarian, and I think it's a country or place that would just about suit anybody's needs. On the whole continent there can be found some place you enjoy particularly for some reason. If you have a chance to travel that much.

Of course you probably know about Liberia where they encountered all kinds of problems between the so-called American Liberians and the native folk. Do you think that this type of problem would develop again if substantial numbers of Black Americans came here to settle again?
Are you talking about a specific incident? You mean the people who went there, that group?

Yes, a lot of people feel that the native people have been exploited and kept out of the power structure. Most of the people who occupy the higher positions of political power are from the United States, Afro-Americans who came there in the 1820s and the 1830s. Therefore a lot of the native people will rise up and try to gain power from the Black colonialists. So do you think that type of thing could possibly happen if a large number of Black Americans came here? What types of things would you suggest in preparing themselves? Knowing our people and the types of hang-ups they have. What types of things would have to undergo change before they could fit in here and not cause any problems to the native?
I don't think that could happen again. I don't think history would repeat itself in that way again because the situation was so different. In other words, when the ex-slaves went back to Liberia they had definite advantages over native people, and I don't think there is the same type of disparity in education in power now. I think the problems that exist in Liberia between the haves and the have nots among the Black rulers and the masses of the people also exist in a lot of other countries, of course, for different reasons.

If a large number of Afro-Americans did come here to settle, how do you think they would be accepted by the people?
Well, it would depend on a lot of things. I think it should be a slow process and not that sudden because I don't think any one country could absorb an influx of Black Americans. I think there would be few

problems with the people themselves if they came and they were the right kind who wanted to be a part of the country. I feel the people would accept them. It depends on how much assistance the government would give them, how much encouragement, and what their attitudes towards them would be, because any time a family or individual settles in another country, there are problems and they may need assistance. You would expect them to and it depends on whether the government really has a policy in being helpful or not.

Speaking specifically of Kenya in 1965, the whole question came up to the Kenyan parliament whether Afro-Americans should be given instant citizenship here and the Kenyan government voted it down. The late Tom Mboya had some specific comments to say about that. Generally he said that he would discourage the immigration of Black Americans to Africa for all kinds of reasons. For instance, one is the Afro-Americans don't really understand the fundamentals of African culture. When Black Americans come over here, they want to buy sandals made out of car tires. He said that they misunderstand the reasons why Africans wear sandals made out of tires, that it stems from poverty.

Yes, I read what he wrote, in fact, I was in Europe at the time, and my sister sent me the articles from the *Times*. I disagree with practically everything he said and think that one of the problems is that too many Black officials in African governments speak for political reasons. They make statements that I find very discouraging and sometimes actually damaging as far as relationships between Black Americans and Africans are concerned. And, Kenya in particular is very involved with the United States, and I do not believe that America wants Black people to go to Africa. Kenya does want the American dollar so I wouldn't expect him to make a statement any different from that he made. But I can say that I don't think that he actually believed that I still disagree with his whole premise, especially the comments he made about the Afro hairdos. I thought that was pretty ridiculous. I don't think that he really understood the style, which I feel originated as an American style. Not trying to be Africans, but trying to be natural, wearing our hair as it naturally is. His attitude was that they were trying to be African and that Africans didn't wear their hair out like that. This is true except now they are wearing their hair like the Afro-Americans. It's such a shallow issue because basically to most people it's a matter of style.

One other comment that strikes me, made by Africans, is that when Afro-Americans come here they stick together a lot. Do you think that is a bad policy? Do you feel that if more Afros came here, they should assimilate with the people more or should they stay to themselves?

I think it is not good. If you leave home, you have to leave home. You can try to leave home without ever leaving; that's what a lot of White Americans do. I can understand it also because naturally you are related to people you have a lot in common with. But I don't think you should limit yourself to other Americans because you lose a lot out of the whole experience of living in Africa if you do that.

You have certainly immersed yourself with Africans by living in the country and not being in the company of too many Afro-Americans. Do you think that has been a rewarding experience?

I think it has, yes.

When you came to Africa did you have many of the misconceptions of African life that most Afro-Americans get by looking at TV, Tarzan, etc. or did you have pretty good ideas of what life would be like when you got here?

I think I had a good idea because before my first trip I spent a lot of time reading everything I could get my hands on. I had many African friends in the States. In fact about ten years before I left there were times when I had more African friends than Afro-American ones in the United States. So I think I had a good idea of what it would be like.

Do you feel like an African or American or Afro-American?

I definitely feel like an Afro-American if you mean the same thing by that word that I do. I don't think a Black person can be an American. The term Afro-American to me means a separate people, living in America who have common experience, and no matter where I live, even in Europe, I felt that I wasn't an American and it was difficult explaining that to a lot of people. For instance, in England I had a long conversation with an Englishman, and it was a very frank conversation really. We were visiting his home, and we talked for quite a while and he tried to convince me that I was an American. When I came to Africa, he had been to East Africa himself. In fact his brother is married to an African here. He said that I would feel more American than African and that is a statement, attitude, or opinion that I have heard over and over again. The reason this opinion has appeared so often is because that is what White people want to believe. I don't believe it is true, not in my case anyway.

Do you think that, with time, you will begin to feel like an African?

Well, see, I think that to a certain extent I'll always be an Afro-American. My earlier experiences can never be blotted out. Those are the things that formed me and made me what I am, so I'll never lose that. As far as feeling African is concerned, feeling that this continent belongs to me, with time. It just so happens that my relatives didn't run fast enough, but it doesn't matter what happens to me here, good or bad. I don't believe anyone can take that away from me. That is what I believe, that this continent belongs to me as a Black person, no matter where they are, South America, Europe, the United States. They should have the same feeling that they have certain rights based on their heritage which is very strong.

Would you say that you are making an excellent, fair, or good living here?

Oh, in monetary value it is very poor, absolutely no comparison. But how you can live on what you are able to make and the amount of satisfaction you get out of a few shillings I think can go greater. There is less pressure. You can't afford a lot of things, but you don't want them. You don't actually need them and can do very well without them. If those things are that important to you then you shouldn't come unless you are making money like the Europeans.

Materialism to a lot of bloods at home is a pretty thing. They like their clothes, shorts, and the whole thing. I'm curious as to how you put all those things aside and came to that decision?

Mainly because it is easy to put them aside once you have them and you know you can get more. You start asking questions, which I think is what young Whites are doing today in the States. I think that is what the whole hippie thing is about, they start asking themselves what else is there? I just felt that there was nothing else I could work for that I wanted. The main thing that I had wanted after high school I either had or knew that I could get very easily so they no longer meant that much to me to bother about getting. But belonging and being a part of something and being able to contribute something—this wasn't possible to get in the States.

Even the very active work you were doing in the Black community wasn't enough progress?

No, because I consider that whole relationship between Blacks and Whites in America an obscene relationship, and I just didn't want to be part of it. It was a game that two groups had to play—the Whites play white and the Blacks play nigger. I think it had gone on so long that it is necessary for the White man, and that is why he wants the Blacks to stay there. I felt that my work in the States was of some benefit, and I did make some contribution in the States. After a while it wasn't enough for me personally although I think I helped a lot of people. It got to the point where I wanted something for myself, and I also felt that what I was doing was in the long run really not helping anyone because the only thing you could do in the States, as far as work, was to help people adjust to the system. You don't really change anything and I feel it has to be changed.

So would you say that was the case with most civil rights groups and active Black rights groups in the States, that they are of a reformist nature and not necessarily revolutionary?

Yes, and where I disagree with all of them is in their major premise and the idea that America is their home and they have a stake in the country. The country has an obligation to them, and they should stay and get what's due to them. All that is true but impossible.

Some Blacks believe that if we participate in the political process we could have Black mayors and governors and hopefully a president, then things would get better some day. You don't share that belief though?

No. I think things are getting worse at a more rapid rate. Disparity between Black and White is increasing—not decreasing.

Do you have any comment on the drug situation in the United States?

That is another big question. I'm just glad that is now affecting the Whites also. It has been used and is being used as means of holding Black communities in check, because as long as the young are involved in drugs they can't be involved in fighting for anything. As long as it only affects the Black communities, nothing would ever be done about it. I'm not too sure anything will be done about it anyway. But it is great that it is being brought home to the White community increasingly.

What do you envision the future of Africa to be?

I'm really uncertain. I don't believe that the future will be good unless there is more unity within Africa, and the problem with that is unity among Africans is exactly the opposite of what most of the industrial countries who have a financial stake in Africa want. I believe they would do everything to hinder any unity. Whether Africans will succeed in uniting, I don't know!

What do you envision in the future of Afro-Americans?

I think it's a pretty bleak future. I think there will be more and more political games, but as long as the majority of the people believe that their only future is in the United States, I think that will limit the future for the people there. They have to become more international minded and develop more contacts with more Black people around the world.

You certainly traveled around the world. How much have you done?

Well, I've been overseas for about two-and-a-half years now.

Do you find a difference between White Americans and Europeans?

Oh, there is a difference. But one feeling that has come into all White people is the feeling of racial superiority. And that's true in places I've visited and lived as in the States. But that actual day-to-day relationships are different. For instance in Europe they have their history of the slavery and discrimination, but they haven't had large numbers of Blacks so they don't have that guilt feeling the White Americans have. And a lot of the pain the Blacks suffer is due to the guilt that the Whites feel, so the relationship between Blacks and Whites in Europe is very often a better and freer one. I also think because of culture differences between Europeans and White Americans I can understand why many Africans go to Europe and live and raise their families and live pretty complete lives in Europe, in spite of being Black in a White country.

A lot of so-called Black intellectuals debate over the whole questions of whether the major problem in the United States is economic or racial. Whether the major evil is the capitalist system or whether it is racism in the hearts and minds of White folk?

I definitely think it is racial. All you have to do is look at the White laborer or blue-collar worker in the States, and he'll suffer economically and allow himself to be exploited economically as long as he can remain a certain position above the Blacks. White power structure uses him because they know that his basic feelings will be racial and not economic.

I see you brought your children with you. Did they come to the same conclusions themselves about leaving the United States or did you have a lot to do with it?

I think I must have had a lot to do with it because I'm sure that having me for a mother would be impossible for them not to have been influenced by what I've said. The books I have read that they have also read. My friends and comments they have heard. So I think that all of that influences them. But I don't believe at the beginning anyway the feeling was as strong as it was with me because they didn't know as much from experience as I did.

RENEE NEBLETT[1]
SEPTEMBER 22, 1998

Could you please state your name, Renee?

Okay, I always sign my name, "Renee, C. Neblett." "C" is for Cheetham,

[1]Name has not been altered.

my maiden name. And I live in Accra, Ghana, in the section called LaBone. And I have a school at the small village of Copahete.

Could you please spell "LaBone"?
L-A-B-O-N-E.

Where did you live before you went to Africa? And where were you educated?
I was in Boston. I returned to Boston in 1984, after ten years in Düsseldorf, West Germany. I went to school at U. Mass. I went to Goddard College, and I went to Germany to Düsseldorf, where I went to the Quincy Academy and received the equivalent of a bachelor's or master's of fine arts.

So you spent ten years in Germany?
Yes.

Was that primarily as a student?
I went there, you know, after kind of coming off the activism of the '60s and '70s, with the intention of studying. It took me a year to get enough language under my belt, and then I studied for about six years, and then stayed a few years more. While I was there, I worked as a free artist, and I taught at the International School.

And when you were in Germany, did you have any sense that ultimately, you would go to Africa and leave the United States?
I think while I was in Germany, it was more, there was an even more clear ambition. I always tell people that I left America at the end of, as I say, this kind of period of social activism, with a lot of questions. And the wonderful thing about being in Germany in those days, which was very different, there was a very homogeneous . . .

And what were the years in Germany?
It was '74 to '84. What was interesting is that people used to approach me in the streets, Germans and even other Africans, and they'd always ask me where I was from. There was an assumption that, maybe, I was an Ethiopian or a Somalian, or maybe even a Faute from Ghana. And for me, that was a wonderful experience. It was the first time in my life that I had my physical presence suggest to somebody that I was something other than a national problem, that I, in fact, was associated with a culture and a country. So I found that very exciting, although I can frankly say that from the time I was a child, and evidenced, I think, by a piece of writing that I did when I was twelve years old, that my mother still has, I always thought of going to Africa.

Since twelve. And what was there at twelve years of age that made you think you would want to go to Africa?

I think, well, my grandfather, you know. I used to hear talk of Gavi, and I say in those days, it's interesting, because I think there was a kind of "intelligentsia." And I knew who Monroe Trotter was; I knew who Du Bois was. And in after school programs, these were common names in my house.

And I can remember, even discussions of my grandfather being disappointed that nobody helped Ethiopia's Haile Selassie when the Italians were invading. I just remember those kinds of discussions. And I can remember, too, one time, my cousin and I, in those days, we were in predominately White schools. And he was in the top bunk and I was on the bottom, and I can remember one time, we must have been about ten or so, asking, "I wonder how come some people are born Black? I wonder if God just has a bunch of children up there and kind of does 'Eenie, meenie, miney, moe, you're this one, you're Black, you're this one.' " I just wondered, "Why me?"

And my cousin leaped, exposed me at the dinner table. And, in fact, I had those kinds of questions in my head. And my mother and my aunt were so appalled that they went on this real deliberate campaign to make me know that God had made people like a garden of beautiful flowers. And they were even more deliberate in making sure I knew as much Black history or African history as was possible from their knowledge.

So one thing I used to always do, I was always artistic, I used to like to draw. And my mother bought me a set of encyclopedias, and I used to always look at Africa, and I can remember the little paper I did on Africa was on how artistic African people are.

And how old were you when you did this paper?

Twelve. It was an extra credit piece I did for my history class, or geography, or something. I remember having a ballpoint pen, drawing pictures of Africa. And essentially, when I look at it today, I still have it, that paper, all I did was copy the names of all the Europeans who were running Africa. (*Laughter*) Because that's all they had were the names of the countries and the governors of those countries, you know, Livingston and that's all I wrote. But the part that struck, that made the largest impact, it was the picture of the African down carving artifacts. And that's what I focused my whole piece on.

Now how large a family do you come from?

I'm an only child. I was raised with all extended cousins, so I wasn't raised as an only child, but I'm my mother's only child.

And I understand you have two children.
I do, a son and a daughter.

And have they ever been to Africa?
Oh yeah. My son is Sékou. I conceived him in Guinea in '71 when we were there. And, in fact, I named him Sékou because I was at a dinner and in those days we were traveling with Michael and Miriam Makeba, and we were at a dinner with the president, Sékou Touré, in Conakry. And I could barely eat. And so the president, of course, inquired, "Why is she eating so little? She's like a petit wazungu."

So Makeba said to him, "She's expecting a child." And so he looked at me, this incredibly handsome pitch-black man, white robes, you know, I was a young woman, twenty-four, and he kind of leaned over and looked directly in my face with those piercing eyes and asked me if I had a son, what would I name him. And without thinking, I said, we'd name him Sékou. (*Laughter*) And then of course, I looked at Chico, my husband, and he agreed, we'd name him Sékou, and we, in fact named him Sékou after Sékou Touré.

And how old is Sékou now?
He's twenty-six.

And your daughter's name?
Sukari, S-U-K-A-R-I, which is a Swahili word for sugar.

So how much time have they spent in Africa with you?
Sukari's spent the most time. She went to school there for two years and she comes back frequently. I mean, she sees that as a home base, since I've been there now off and on for the last nine years. And Sékou has come a couple of times to visit. And before that, we had traveled in West Africa. When Sékou graduated from high school, we took a three-month trip through West Africa, the three of us did.

And what are some of the African countries you've traveled through?
I've been in West Africa, you know, Ivory Coast, Guinea, Sierra Leone, Liberia, Nigeria, Ghana, Upper Volta. I've been to South Africa. I'm on my way to Addis Ababa next week. That's about it—mostly west and south.

And have you met many African-Americans in these countries who've decided to leave America and to go there and live?
Yes, I have.

Approximately how many?
Well, Ghana has a substantial number. It's a very interesting time in

Ghana, as it was, apparently a very interesting time about thirty years ago, during independence, because there's a legacy, there's an old African-American community in Ghana that have been there for years. In fact they're in their late seventies and eighties now. They went there during independence. And I know there's large colonies or substantial groups that went to Tanzania, Algeria. There's also an interesting community in South Africa.

But more and more African-Americans, how large, I can't say. There's a couple thousand, I think, in Ghana.

Now by being in Africa, what do you miss most about America?

I guess the obvious things to say are certain conveniences, but I don't really, really miss those things. I mean, on occasion, I think I miss museums or theater on occasion. But I travel enough so that it doesn't. I don't really feel the loss of it, or the absence of it. I guess that's what I miss. To be quite honest, I'm rather content there.

A number of people that I've spoken to, African Americans in Africa, said that they missed the music and the culture of America, soul music, dancing, jazz, those kinds of things. Does that bother you at all?

What I find interesting is that I think, if anything, that's the thing that endears Africa to me, is all the music and the dancing, this kind of constant, ever-present part of life. I think what I like, in fact, is the kind of cohesiveness, the constant celebration of "Africa-ness" and "Negritude." I mean, now with Clinton, I think for the first time that I can remember, that African-American culture has been afforded a kind of public forum in the context of a rather popular American culture, rather than a kind of addendum or something people do in dark, dank places.

And in contrast, it doesn't matter what the occasion, whether a fetish priest is being inaugurated or a baby is being born, or the president's coming, you have the same intense, vibrating, clearly African music. And that's what I like, it's everywhere. It has a place in the entire life of that community. When the president comes, everybody's going to dance, you know.

Everyone?

Everyone. I mean, if I'm honest, I remember as a child, there was a kind of grooming that we received, you know, answers we had, we weren't really allowed to let White people know. If White people inquired, "What kind of music do you like?" I was supposed to say, "I like all kinds of music," and I was supposed to make sure they knew that I couldn't dance or sing. (*Laughter*) There were no pat ways. I'm not sure if people sat me down, but it was clear that there were certain things you were supposed to say, so that you distinguished yourselves from the path of Negroes around. (*Laughter*) I remember those things.

And in contrast, in Africa, you don't have to do that. There's not a constant systematic way, that everything has some reference and negritude is not assigned a kind of "second class" place. I remember, for example, when Jesse Jackson gave that great speech, when he was running for president. And all the reporters could do was to say, "Well, in the tradition of the old Negro sermon," as though by describing it that way, they were qualifying it as less than whatever Cuomo or whoever did, rather than celebrating that wonderfully rich oratorical tradition. So that's the kind of constant thing that I am happy not to be part of.

Now has your conception of America changed as a result of being in Africa?

I mean, I guess I do think sometimes more positively about America. I do think that there really is a great opportunity, if seized, that America really is about, without sounding cliché, it really has the possibility, it's like Atlantic, you know, whatever you think of that, to be a wonderfully rich, diverse place. I think there are a lot of things we have here that we take for granted. I mean, sometimes, I do crave different foods. You know, people in most of the world are happy with whatever their staple diet is—that's what they crave. I can crave Chinese food one day and Italian the next, and wish I can have hummus another day, and tabouli. You really forget how broad a palate this incredibly diverse land has afforded you. And so when I think of it that way, when I think of the incredibly tremendous potential, I have hopes for America.

But it's funny, my experience in Ghana is a bit different from living in Europe. When I lived in Europe, I clearly felt as though I was there, but I felt really uninvolved, happily uninvolved. I mean, after the early activism, I was happy to have my peace. And I think it was Bertolt Brecht that said, "Man understands himself best in estrangement." And in Germany, I did. I was able to think about who I was and I was able to think about America, who I was in America and who I was in a kind of international community. And there were a lot of revelations.

In Ghana, it's a little bit different because I'm not Ghanaian, obviously. But I do feel as though I am a tribe of the African world, albeit an African-American, which I think is a distinct tribe, distinguished by its miseducation, distinguished by all the experiences that have taken this particular cross-section of Africans and shaped them into a kind of a unique entity.

And I feel very, I want that to be articulated. I really want that to be, I want the African-American experience to be defined, preserved, and celebrated as an important cultural historic entity. And I think, coming back today, when there's so much integration, you have Haitian-Americans, and you have first and second generations of Africans who are migrating, you know, they are not African-Americans.

I'm talking about those of us on the mainland, those of us who are descendants of Africans who were enslaved on this continent, and whose unique experience made the blues out of misery and a delicacy out of swine. I want that institutionalized, who seized European forms to express African ideas and, in the process of doing that, have created whole new entities. I want us to articulate, seize that, you know, from June teenth days to our Kwanza. It should be our intellectuals, it should be working feverishly to institutionalize those things, before we end up like other tribes, and that is extinct as a cultural entity.

Now do you see, by being in Africa, you help to perpetuate this type of history that you just described? Or can someone interpret it as sort of giving up on the African-American?

No. I mean the reason I went to Ghana and what I'm doing there is I went there to start a school. And I have started a school, and the goal of that was to create an American institution in Africa that provided the opportunity for discipline-based academic learning, and obviously the arts are a part of that, that acknowledged Africa in general, West Africa in particular, as an old world to the Americas, and by doing that, afforded students, all students, American students and Ghanaian, a chance to not only expand the material basis of what they've learned, because I'm always amazed, I don't care what schools they go to, Harvard, Yale, Princeton, they don't even know why the Americas are the Americas.

Everybody here is so smart and they have no sense of who we are in this world. Their sense of geography and who the Americas are, what has happened to the migration of people, what people, the difference between a Spanish or an English colony or a French colony or a Portuguese colony, or a colony of Africans, they have no clue.

And I wanted to create an institution, to create a direct link to those resources to American education. And as an African-American woman, we come from a long tradition. I mean that is the thing that distinguishes us. Unfortunately, what distinguished us is that we're not in control of writing our own history and articulating who we are in this world, but the fact is that we were building institutions a half a step out of slavery.

And so I think it's only fitting, and I was blessed to have the experiences I've had, so that I can see that link. And there's a range of experiences that took me to this place. I mean, movement, being raised by educators, having people like Mrs. Snowden and Ms. Lewis and my mother in my life. Mrs.

Nurse, people who cared about education coming up, as I said, when traveling with Makeba and Carmichael, and Rap Browns and my former husband, Chico Neblett, you know, getting abroad, teaching in an international school system, public school system, coming back here and finding myself in an elite private school, getting a chance to see another whole culture, that people, as a matter of course, take semesters abroad, and you know, create schools like Mountain Schools where kids can actually go and live and work on a working farm for a semester so they can have another relationship with nature. All of these experiences helped me to imagine the possibilities that could exist with creating that kind of linkage and how it could work.

So the school is called Kokrobitey School. And who is the co-founder with you, co-visionary?

The co-visionary, Alero Olympio. Her name is there because Alero, actually, I met Alero some seven years after I started the initiative. What Alero did was help me physically build it. And we now have a physical plant that can house forty people, has a lovely dining area, seminar hall, classroom accommodation, on a splendid site, and she helped take this idea and transform it into a visual reality to something that's real life. And not just in a functional way, but aesthetically, it's really lovely.

As an African that's Ghanaian, was she able to give you certain insights that, perhaps, you would not have as an African-American, into, as far as the design of the school, the physical design of the school, as well as the curriculum?

Okay, she had little to do with the curriculum. With the design of the school, I mean, what's unique about Alero is that she is interested in building in natural materials. And unfortunately, most Africans, all they want to do is copy something they've seen in Switzerland or France. And as long as there's plenty of cement and large indoor spaces with little windows, which is completely in contradiction to their own cultural reality and the physical environment they're in. That's what they go for.

So I was fortunate, I was walking around with a little drawing that I had in my pocket and how I saw it working, what I had hoped. And when I met Alero, the thing that impressed me was that she was the very first architect I spoke to that said to me, when I showed her the designs, she said, "Wait a minute, tell me the whole idea, what are you trying to do? Tell me the whole vision."

And so then I gave her the whole idea, and at the end, she said, "You want a sacred place, a sacred space to learn and to be." And from that point on, I tell people it was like cooking with my best friend. I mean, the instincts that she had, I mean, not only her skills as a builder and contractor, I mean she designs and builds furniture so she's completely practical, and a result of her sensibilities, I was trying to, I heard about this building, and it was just coincidental. We met right at the same time, and I had, the day I met her, I said, "Well I know somebody who's actually building a place. I saw a house someplace, my driver had shown me some weeks ago, because I've been talking about it."

And my driver said, "I think I've seen something like what you want." And so I took Alero and she said, "Wow, this is amazing." And so we went and found this guy, we found the machine, and we actually produced bricks, over 6,000 bricks a day for over a month. We produced our own bricks, we were able to organize the local villages as a labor force, we hired the women to procure the rocks and the stones with which we build the structures.

And we built off the skills that we saw there. And there's not a great tradition in building in wood in Ghana. So we had to be very creative. And we cut out a lot of expenses by acting as contractor, practically living there and using people who were absolutely unskilled in very creative ways. Alero is an extraordinary architect and builder. And so it was, as well, an opportunity for her, to have met somebody who would give her free reign really.

Now you referred to the place as a "sacred place." Sacred in what sense?

Well, when you think of places to study, in the Eastern tradition, they called learning, "sacred places of learning," the idea of courtyards and colonnades and private spaces and individual places and beauty. I mean we can look around and see, you can go to a public institution that's a city block long, massive cinder blocks and little tiny windows, and then you go to the private schools or high schools that they make with their rolling fields and tables and people in different manners in different spaces.

Are you a citizen of Ghana?

No, I'm a resident right now. But I hope to receive dual citizenship. There's a referendum to afford African-Americans dual citizenship.

In Ghana?

Yes.

And how far along is that?

It's reasonably far along. I mean, I think in the next year or two, there should be some closure in that. You've had, you know, with Du Bois, especially with the independence within Cuba. I mean Cuba was really influenced by the likes of Garvey and Du Bois, and he was a real Pan-Africanist. And he saw the wealth of resource, and the need for Africans in the Americas to not only be allowed a chance to repatriate, to have a homeland, but he also understood what skills and resources their experiences in the Americas afforded them, and what a resource they potentially could be.

Now, where is Du Bois buried?
Accra—within walking distance of my house.

Is there a nice monument to him?
There is a lovely monument. He and his second wife Shirley are buried there, and they've built a lovely . . . it's not just a monument. I mean, he lays in state there.

What do you like best about Africa and Ghana in particular?
Well, Ghana is a very special place in Africa; it's one of the few places that still is very African. I mean, the Ghanaian people are extraordinarily friendly. And curiously enough, there are so many things, you know, when I think of my childhood life in the '50s, there are so many things that I see in Ghana that are familiar to me. Everybody is "Auntie" and "Uncle," you know. You never go to anybody's home where they don't offer you, first, something to drink, and then, something to eat.

That's the way we used to be here in the '50s. There's a certain quality and gentility, a certain level of what I've learned to call symbolic gesture, which is just good manners. That's the kind of constant element of life. Everybody understands standing to greet another human being, it just is a symbolic gesture. It's not an imposition on their individual right, taking your hat off if you're at the dinner table or putting it on, whatever the case may be. It distinguishes that activity from maybe, digging a ditch or being in a football field. It's just a symbolic gesture.

So what I like is that you still have a society that agrees on systems of expressing their values. And I find that very comforting. I like those kinds of rituals. And aside from the friendliness. Well, Ghana, as well as I said, besides being friendly, is African. There's Kwame Nkrumah. There's Du Bois Place. There's Blackstal Square. There's Marcus Garvey. There's George Padmore Library. I mean you're living in the presence of great men who are African people. And it's okay.

So you get a sense that Ghana recognized Pan-African contributions of Africans in diaspora. Is this being reflected in the curriculum of the schools in Ghana?
Interestingly enough, that has kind of died away. And there's a bit of a crisis, in fact, because all of a sudden, America is very interested in Ghana. And that's why I smiled a bit when you said, do I miss their music? I mean

there's this incredible effort, the CNNs and all that, to transport a certain type of African-American culture, whatever, "Snoopy-Doggy-Dog" whatever that genre is.

And we know alongside them, in every African community, there are cultural dance groups, and the Taj Mahals of this generation who are doing incredible things. We never hear about them. And I think there's a debate going on now where some Ghanaians, obviously, some of them, they don't care. American means more prosperity, they get a car, house, they could care less. They put a baseball cap on their kid's head backwards, thinking they're emulating prosperity. And before they know it, they'll be in the same critical condition we find ourselves in, socially. So there's a debate going on now. I mean, the president speaks about it, there are intellectuals who are concerned about the maintenance of African culture, the sustenance of it.

But there are also other issues too. It's very complex. Obviously, we have to see African culture as dynamic. There's a part, especially from those of us in the diaspora that hold tight to something that's ancient and naive and simple and pure. And you know, that's nice, but that's also not reflective of development and reality. And there is a great need for African culture to mature on its own. Part of why we see that kind of stagnant situation is a result of all kinds of disruption or people have been under siege.

Africans are a conquered people. And as a result, many things have been thwarted, not just their economy. But I think it's one of the natural ways culture has evolved. And I hope that it's not going to jump, the same way the economy has been forced to jump from the Stone Age into whatever else, the Technological Age or somebody else's industrial revolution. I hope that's not going to happen culturally. If anything, in that respect, I think the African diaspora has a role to play.

Now are these cultural changes, changes that you describe, the influence of American "hip hop" culture on African culture, I would guess that that's occurring primarily within the cities, that in the villages that they're immune from that kind of influence?

Well, I mean, only as immune as they are from having access to technology. Of course, you still have villages that don't have electricity. I don't have electricity where I am. That doesn't mean that people don't hook up batteries to their radio and get the same transmission being sent in. And again, I've learned a lot about hip hop. Unlike some years ago when I thought I just had no understanding for the constant staccato four-letter words, I do find something in the form these days. So it's not just the hip hop. It's the type that's being sold that's out of our hands.

I mean it's the same thing that's happening to religion over there. I mean all of a sudden, you have a deluge of Christian churches, everything, even the Mormons are there staking a claim.

Are they primarily in the cities, or in the countryside as well?

They're going where they can. They're there, Latter-Day Saints, and then, there's this kind of evangelistic, there's the Anglo-European American who's copied this African-American style of ministry. And of course, Ghanaians are not like African-Americans—they've not been oppressed. They don't have the same feeling or experiences with White people that we've had. So they're not cautious instinctively, fortunately, for them, in some ways, that they haven't had their whole reality diced up in that kind of way. But I'm saying that to say there's an incredible naivety.

Now what about the traditional religions? Are they still flourishing?

Oh, there's a few in small pockets, and people are working feverishly to condemn them. I mean, there's a whole big thing now, they're talking about slavery, everything is slavery now. There may have been tradition where a certain group of girls were in line to marry chiefs, and what they call virgin priestesses, and somebody comes and looks at that tradition and says, "Oh, she doesn't have a choice," and so that institution is wrong and she's a slave.

And it's a bit more complex than that. But that's how they're reducing it to that kind of Black-White equation. And they're beating these people up. And what it means is that churches won't come into your community and build a school. So if you hold onto those things, you will suffer. And they're doing that vigorously. They're trying the best they can to wipe out, and the Christian churches . . . (*inaudible*) I mean it's amazing to watch in this day and age, just how a people's culture can be so wiped out.

Last night I was watching television and they had a rabbi. They were showing a traditional Jewish service on the opening of the celebration of Rosh Hashanah. And they showed the rabbi with the long cow's horn calling in the high tones. And that's what they do in traditional Ghanaian religion. And I thought what's wrong with African people, we can't hold onto nothing? But that's what they do with the horns and they sing it.

And the other day, when I was at a reception in New York, I was very happy that a couple of the Council of Chiefs were in from Ghana, and a couple of the Queen Mothers, and they actually got in and they said, "We're pouring libations. This is the way the African, the Ghanaian expresses his acknowledgment of God. It is not demonistic; we're not fighting the Christians. We're only holding onto the traditions of our fathers." And he went on and poured libation and everybody clapped. So I was glad to hear that some-body's picking this up.

Well, increasingly, we see that in the United States among academics.

Well, good. What I'm saying to you is that the African and the diaspora is going to be a key player in how much of traditional African society is main-tained. We are pivotal.

It's interesting that you see those in the Diaspora as being key, as opposed to the Africans themselves, protecting their culture.

Well, obviously we'll take leadership from the intelligentsia they've managed to nurture. But there's no question that we have a broader base of intelligence, even those who are not intellectuals, that have a sense of the importance of holding onto their cultural belongings.

We don't take them for granted. And, in fact, you have people there that just take it for granted. And they think the progress is getting rid of that raffia skirt now, and they've got their Nike sneakers on. That's progress. And we know that there's a space in between those two. It doesn't have to be either/or.

Well, last year, there was a lot in the press about clitorectomy.

Female circumcision.

Right. And the idea the press was putting forth was that it deprived the Afri-can woman of her sexuality and that it was a form of sexism and control over the women. What's your take on that?

To be honest, I don't know enough about it. I really don't. I don't know. I mean whatever my intellectual African-American female friends who are feminists, you have to subscribe, the whole nine yards, to the notion that you're a feminist. I'm not a feminist. I don't understand it. It's too complex to me. But I'm sure there's no question that there can be some things that are, if it's just inflicting pain and really depriving someone of pleasure, and it's done in ways that are completely unsanitary, there's obviously cause for concern. I don't know enough about it.

Now in Ghana, how far are you from Accra the capital?

The school? About twenty kilometers.

And in mileage, what's that?

Thirty-six miles, maybe. Maybe not that far, actually. Maybe fifteen kilo-meters, about thirty miles.

Have you run across many African-Americans within that area who are engaged in businesses?

Sure.

And what kinds of businesses are they involved in?

Well, as a whole, America's always very clever, and part of the power is that there's some of everything here. So whenever she goes into a country, she can always put some of those country's own people there . . . (*laughter*) to work for her. So there's a number of African-Americans, obviously, in the diplomatic court these days. But outside of that, there's the older African-Americans I know there, and some have a hotel. These are older women who are married, and most of these people are married to Ghanaians now.

What's the name of the hotel?

(*Pause*) It will come to me.

And those African-Americans who are in diplomatic corps, do they interact very much with, say, people like yourself, who are there on your own?

They do. I mean they see themselves as kind of high, privileged, or whatever. I mean if we meet on the street there are some of them, they're brothers and sisters on some level, the same you find here, they think they just died and gone to heaven talking to you, well-formed, clipped syllabic ways.

But then there are other African-Americans. There's my sister Mona Boyd who has a really flourishing travel agency and car rental. In fact, she handled all the vehicles when President Clinton came. She coordinated that whole effort. And there are some people like Dr. Lee who is a dentist from, I think he went to Tuskegee, no, not Tuskegee, Lincoln University. And Cuomo went to Lincoln.

So you get that whole slew. And as I said, there are other old African-American women, one who had just married a Ghanaian man who owned their first chicken farm. There was another African-American sister, Blanche, who's married to a Ghanaian. And another sister who runs a thriving bakery. Every Ghanaian wants a Blanche cake at their party.

And now you're getting new entrepreneurs. I mean whenever I watch the television, there's a constant delegation of African-Americans coming over there. And some of them I haven't met, but I know there's one brother and sister who just bought X-amount of acres and they're trying to farm rice. And there's an older couple down in Cape . . . (*inaudible*) out of New York, who really do a thing with the castles, this idea of the past, all the ritual. They're Africans.

And then I don't mind saying there are a whole bunch of "riffraff" running around, everybody, trying to get a job here, get a ticket, and get over there and doing the roots thing.

Now what's the roots thing?

Whatever it is, living hand-to-mouth. And in some ways, I think that's a problem. I think it's unfortunate that you have to find ways to control society. Ghana is not an economy that can just absorb people who do nothing.

Out of the African-Americans who are there, this latter group you just described, the so-called "riffraff"—

Let me just say that there are a bunch of people there that are just kind of searching around.

So that group, what percentage are they of the total African-American population?

I'm not sure. Because some of them could live in remote areas and in a kind of commune and here and there. I'm not really sure.

Now do you find that you've been accepted as a returned sister?

On some levels. Some levels, I may just be seen as a White woman, you know. I think what I'm doing with the school obviously affords me a particular position. You ask about Alero, I mean, meeting somebody like Alero was really also an introduction to a whole kind of young intelligentsia. Normally, the children of the generation who were great scholars and writers and Du Boisians and . . . (*inaudible*) And so from that perspective, I found a rather comfortable community. And of course, I'm accepted. And in fact, it's even celebrated that certain African-Americans can return and add their skills—whatever is possible.

In the village, in Kokrobitey, because of the nature of what I'm doing, I enjoy a reasonable status. But of course, there are fishing villages, and some of these people are really ignorant. I'm not saying they're uneducated, but they're ignorant to other things. And I might just represent somebody who has more than they have. And that's why Kokrobitey School makes a concerted effort to work with the chiefs. We invite them to all our functions to make sure that our community service activities evolve around uplifting the local school so that they see us differently.

Now do you find that being a woman is a disadvantage or an advantage in Ghana?

No, I don't. I find some of the most powerful women. If you're capable, you know, people assume their own position in Ghana. It's not unusual for someone to say, "Hey, that's a big woman, Auntie." It means she does her thing. And people respect that. If you do what you do, it has to do with your own energy and persona. And needless to say, I'm not going to say that women are not, in any society where you're unable to take care of yourself, then you find yourself at the mercy of others. And that's why I'm a little cautious about going the whole nine yards with whatever feminism is supposed to be. Juanita Hill, is that her name?

Anita Hill.

Anita Hill. I thought she was a national disgrace, quite frankly. I can't imagine, I mean, somebody starts telling you dirty jokes, and you subject yourself to listening to it, and then you follow that one person, and she has ten brothers and sisters and she doesn't tell anybody.

How could our Department work to support your school?

Obviously, there's a whole range of disciplines that could be interesting, to make a whole semester of studying. How it would work is that the institution, or it could come from a consortium of institutions, would send over one professor. That professor would teach two courses.

The institution would work with Kokrobitey to define and design a course of study, so if, say, you sent somebody who was an environmental scientist and was going to teach two courses, and you taught somebody, you sent somebody who was a historian who was going to teach two courses, then we could decide what the rest of the curriculum would have to look like. Say, "Okay, we need an English course, we need an archaeology course, or we need whatever."

The Kokrobitey school would submit the credentials to people of that field from our adjunct faculty lists, and they would essentially become adjunct faculty of your institution. So the credit is actually cycled through you.

Then there's the whole Kokrobitey piece, well, what else does Kokrobitey offer? Well, we have an independent study, so that if the kids are there, they would have a whole college life, take their core courses, maybe five, and then an independent study. There's a whole component of field trips that support the learning activity. There's community service. There's a sports program. There's a home and village state that all make this life an interesting piece.

And say, you sent twenty students. And they don't all have to come from here. If you opened it up, I know there are people at Rutgers and Eastern Connecticut University who would come if somebody took over getting that information out, state school. They'd come from South Carolina. I get people asking all the time.

Then, say twenty students came from the States; then all I would ask is that we could take up to one fifth, that I could bring in five Ghanaian students who would also live on-campus. So essentially, what you're affording kids in a public institution like U Mass is a private college semester abroad with their Ghanaian counterparts. It's something that doesn't exist; it's a very interesting model.

You could talk about the intimacy of learning, you could talk about living, you know what Kokrobitey is—it's rural. But we're not so far away from the cities that you can't get into the libraries and the cultural and social resources that the urban area has to offer us, but at the same time, you live in that small area fishing villages, where you have a real active experience.

The adjunct faculty come from where?

Yeah, well, I have whole list of people I work with from the University of Meghon and Cape Coast University who are just professionals in various fields. So if you said you wanted an English course, I might say, "Well why don't we try Essie Sutherland?" Or, "Let's have Arnie Hoeder, he's good." Or, "Let's have Amata Edu. She's a published writer; she can teach the English course." And what I can do is get it together and you can take it before the Governing Board here, we as a faculty . . . (*inaudible*) But I have a whole model for this. I've done it with Connecticut College; it's been done before.

Now how many of our faculty would have to do it?

Just one faculty person, and that faculty person would be like the team leader for the semester. You're doing your regular job. So the faculty here, to replace you, maybe you'd hire an adjunct person for that semester to replace you on the faculty to take your courses. But you'd be teaching your full load. You have your two courses, you'd be doing counseling, advising.

What disciplines would you be interested in?

The discipline or the focus can vary, which means you can have a broad appeal. One year, it could be, maybe a focus on environmental science. Maybe that's the person that comes down. The next year it could be government, the person that comes down. Do you know what I'm saying? As well as the rest of the curriculum that we put together.

What would your school offer academically?

We, of course, have a Kokrobitey agenda, an agenda we would work out. We know that the literature programs, that the science teacher came from here, who's going to work with an African scientist and look at how to get the most out of it. But he's coming to a Kokrobitey experience, which means there's going to be an African literature course, there's going to be the archaeology or the history, which is Europe, African, and the pan-American experience.

Those courses would be there. Those are the courses that we would offer and run. And we oversee that. They'd be the homes day and the village day, and there'd still be the field trips. So that you can actually use Kokrobitey as a way to fling out to the broader academic community there, and solicit their participation. Do you see what I'm saying? That's what I'm trying to do with this.

And we're trying to say, "What's the logic in this?" Why would American students, African-American, Anglo-American, Asian-American, find that interesting? Well, aside from your discipline in the sciences, okay, environmental studies, it's interesting. It's an old world. A course there, Europe, Africa and the Pan-American experience, it would be great for American students to take that course. It helps fit in a large piece. Because we want to take advantage of that. What are other ways to look at it?

It's not only old world, which means you still have access to looking at indigenous cultures. It's an emerging economy. A business department could come there, and we could put the kids in independent study and workplaces, as well as a business person teaching two courses in economy, complemented by the adjunct faculty, whoever we decided, whatever those courses would be to support that.

Then there's the whole Kokrobitey agenda. We live a certain way. It's all about the African personality, the way we take our meals, the morning proverb, the field trips we take. There are standard field trips, revisiting the old world, the castles, there's the ancient Ashanti empire, Kumazzi, there's our whole piece when we go to Enzima. There are some standard things that we do.

Do you speak any African languages?
Not really. I understand some Twi and a little Ga.

Some people, in discussing the problem in the United States, say it's primarily a racial problem; some say, it's an economic one, capitalism. I'm sure you have done thinking on that question . . . (Laughter)
Of course. There's no question, let me tell you. I mean, years ago, it was easy. It was a race issue. You never saw a sign that said, "no poor," or "no ignorant." It said, "no niggers, no negroes and no blacks." It was very clearly a race issue. But now it's easier to disguise, but the whole economy of this country was built on race. So now where you don't have to use race, a whole economic reality has been created based on race. So now you can say, "no poor," and know who's the majority of those poor. I mean there's no ques-

tion, I mean, anybody who reads Du Bois, or if you have a pea brain, you know that the whole entire structure of this country is, the economics has been defined and built on race.

Well what about class? What about capitalism? And what role do you see capitalism playing in the development of Africa, if any?

Well, I mean, obviously, what about class? Class is also a product of economics, even though, as an African-American who was raised in Boston, I know there's such a thing as an African-American aristocrat, that really didn't have money, but they had a certain intellectual stature.

But as the world or this civilization matures, if you want to call it that, we know that even class takes its place when it comes to money. Some big illiterate overnight Lotto winner or sports figure or stockbroker junkie manages to make a lot of money, and nobody cares how good his English is. Money is what talks. When I was a kid, people were distinguished by how they made their money. We didn't think the money of a prostitute was the same as somebody who what we thought had honest labor. We were always, "Work for a nickel, but don't take a dime." That's how I was raised. But nobody cares anymore.

A documentary on television a couple weeks ago, where you had Joe Kennedy with the mobsters of those days, they're the same. It doesn't matter. Capitalism, I mean, it's a very interesting thing. What can I say? Right now, America has the money, the capitalist system seems to be wielding all the power. I'm not versed enough in economics.

I just know this: That no one man's labor is worth the labor of a million people. I don't care how late Bill Gates stays up at night, he didn't do anything, having the money he has, when you have another million people who get up every day from sunup to sundown, cannot collectively have the same money he has, something is wrong. That's all I have to say about that. I'm not an economist.

I would also go so far as to say, I remember some years ago, there was a young student, Kwame Toure aka Stokely Carmichael, was lecturing some kids in Ghana, and a young Jewish boy got up, and he kind of reared back on his heels and he said, "Well Mr. Carmichael, it's really interesting to hear you talk about the glories of Cuba and all the other socialist experiments, but the fact is we've just watched the fall of the Soviet Union and watched this dissipate and that, and capitalism, America, is in the height of her days and she's growing dramatically. And surely now you must know that communism is a failure. You have to say that that's a failure."

And he said, "I don't know if I would say that." He said, "I think maybe it hasn't been practiced properly. It's like Christianity. Half the Christians you know don't live up to Christian doctrines, but you don't say the doctrine itself is no good." So that's what I think of.

Now, Africa consciousness. Students in the States kick around the whole issue of Africa consciousness. Should one be concerned, should we see ourselves primarily as Americans? What's the importance of Africa consciousness to African-Americans, particularly students?

It's everything. And I think when I started the whole discussion, I said, there's nothing, so many things sound cliché, but if you don't know where you're coming from, you don't know where you're going. Africa 0consciousness doesn't mean everybody should think about going back to Africa, that you don't have a reality in the moment that you are, that you're not an American. America is a society made up of different people in the world.

We can look at those people and we know the ones who are the strongest. The ones who have a long historical conscience and cultural identity are the strongest people. So we can look at the Jews. It doesn't matter where they find themselves, there's some common denominator. We can look at various Europeans, and I don't care how rich or how poor, their cultural identity has distinguished them, not only culturally but economically.

Case in point, we can go down to East Boston, the Italian community. There's an Italian-American community. People know where they come from, they have certain traditions, they're Americans, nobody disputes that, but they have a cultural and historical conscience. And as a result, even their community, as an ethnic entity, is sustained and celebrated.

Look at the Black Americans, because we can't hold on and define who we are, we can't even point to where Monroe Trotter's house is. We can't even go to the point where the great African-American migration started and to the points where the Africans first settled. We managed to hold onto a few little squares there, Beacon Hill. But because we are not culturally whole, we have no historical reference, we are nothing. Our kids don't even know the difference between spiritual music and gospel music. And because we move with the trends, and now the music is fact, that doesn't mean spiritual music, the very music, that lethargical music that saw us through some of the darkest days that were built not only on the African essence, energy, but the old Judaic tradition of singing freedom and emancipation. All these traditions we pulled on to create this, we don't even have a memory.

We don't even know that Africans, because they took the drum away from us in British colonies, that energy, that need to define ourselves through a cultural memory, said, "Okay, we'll play the spoons and we'll tap dance. We don't even know the traditions that have saved our life. How can we imagine the future? What is Africa?"

And people say, "Oh, you go to Africa, can you speak the language?" African-Americans go back and then they realize they can't speak the language, they can't do this. How can you speak the language of someplace you were taken away from for 500 years? I have found everything in Africa I was looking for. When I go there I see people that look like my grandfather. I found everything I was looking for. I wasn't looking to live in the past—I was looking for a memory. I was looking for the origin of something.

Malcolm said, "If a cat has kittens, do you call them 'biscuits'? No, they're kittens." Just because these Africans were taken from that kind of Africa and born, in Mexico, they're still an African. And what is wrong with us? That is our death; that is our undoing. And the fact is that our history is so illustrious.

Yes, Africans sold other Africans into slavery, yes. But there's no question in anybody's mind. There was long tradition of slavery and indentured servitude. But no African that participated in that had any clue that he was selling those other Africans who, traditionally, could have been sold to another tribe, which they did, which made the tribe larger, eventually married their sons and daughters. They did not know that those people were going to then be considered animals. Make no mistake about it.

You have to know where you came from. There are things that would inform us about what kind of memory caused us, and it wasn't just our moaning. I ask myself all the time, when I think of those Africans that one day found themselves trapped in those dungeons, after being huddled together with people from different languages, complete strangers, found themselves lying in the bottom of ships, lying in their own excrement, and the corpses, for months in the bottom of a vessel, to get up and find themselves on the other side of the world, where for the rest of their born days they would be considered three fifths of a human being, shadowed, bred, mutilated. When I look at that, all I ask myself is what made those people get up in the morning? I just don't know how they could get up. But they did, and I want to know what was the spiritual essence of those lives that allowed them to make the blues out of misery? They did whatever they did so that you and I could sit here today. Because it was obviously something, it wasn't just a physical strength. They came from someplace. There is some cultural reality that forged the temperament and the being of those humans.

Do you think that a substantial number of African-Americans should come to Africa to settle?

I don't know. I mean, I don't think every European has to go back to Italy or France or Spain or Germany. It's their choice. I think more important than going there physically is to spiritually make that trek, whether it's just at your desk or a book, and you're on your knees at prayer. So that you can have the strength to not mind telling people, "Yes, we come from a tradition of people who can sing and dance."

Now when you came to Africa, did you have any of the typical misconceptions about life there that some African-Americans normally have?

Yeah, I think I was surprised that the average African didn't feel as angry towards White people as I did. I think that took me a minute. And I'm saying that in a most general way, because I've lived there. I have very good friends across the ethnic and social and economic spectrum of this reality. I'm not going to cheapen it by saying, "Some of my best friends are . . . " but the fact is, some are.

But the larger piece, from the time I was a small girl, fifteen, sixteen years old, reading about kids being bombed in churches and having high school guidance counselors telling me to go in the army, or people ignoring me when I raised my hand. I mean that was a fact of my life, racism.

So I've always identified masses of White people in relationship to my individual being in an adversarial way. And on when I've found myself in certain situations alone, I was afraid, if I could be honest. The first time I landed in Mississippi, I was afraid. The first time I found myself in South Boston lost, I was afraid. I think, fortunately, going to Europe and getting out of there, being around Europeans, living in Germany, I saw things very differently for a change. All of a sudden there were individual acts of racism, but there wasn't anything quite as institutional as I had experienced here. That was a fact of life.

And so I was amazed, even though I had had little experiences that were priming me to accept and understand that every dark person in the world hadn't had the same conditioning, and, in fact, living with Ghanaians, I was really able to see just how this condition we lived in America had really, I won't say distorted, but altered, our personalities as African-Americans. Because as a group of people, we are more angry, much more skeptical, we're much more on guard. It's just kind of a characteristic of our being. It's a learned behavior. You know, most Africans on the continent are not self-consciously Black. When they say, "Look at that man," they don't say, "Look at that Black man." They say "Look at that man." They don't have to qualify their existence, so there's all these things that make them very different from us.

And in fact, it's a pleasure sometimes, to be around people that have not been conditioned to respond to everything in that way.

So race is deemphasized in Africa.

Yeah. I mean obviously, people are aware that there was a colonial time. But it's not quite the same as, even though there was colonialism, and you had slaves kind of imitating their colonial masters. Actually, it's probably happening more now. Because African-Americans, everyday, "Hi, Liz, Hi John," I mean, it's awful. You can't even tell Black people by the way they speak. If you want to make it, just forget who you are. Close all of that. You want blond hair, be blond. Make sure they can't tell who you are on the phone. Change your voice. It's amazing.

And all you have to do is watch the news, watch these people on television. Who are these people? I was on the train the other day, just to listen to these kids talk, they're Anglo-Americans, because culture is a product of community. Our culture, because of the oppression, race, or color defined us. That's why we can have people who can be almost alabaster or pitch black. Their experience was defined by racism. And so we were all together.

Now, integration has come and broken up, which I think is one of the worst things that has happened to the African-American community. What's happened though is that African-American culture is being completely dispersed, and they're the cultured Anglo-Americans. We are in no position to articulate what's important about who we were or who we are. And so we're just being lost. Just because you're Black doesn't make any difference. If I put you in China, you'd be Chinese, culturally. So I think it's very unfortunate that we are not holding onto eating black-eyed peas on New Year's like folks used to do, and pig's feet . . . (*Laughter*) That's what people did New Year's. They ate black-eyed peas and pig's feet.

And the Jews know that, matzo balls and all, they're not their staple diet. But it has a place in their tradition, on certain days, to remember where they come from.

Now do you feel like an African-American or an American?

I feel like an African-American. And to me, if I said to you an African-American is somebody who can trace their lineage, who's a product of miseducation, who's part of Africans who were brought to the new world, who were, in fact, enslaved here, and any number of experiences they might have gone through, in my case, found themselves in the North and were mixed up with Wompanog Indians. But because of the segregation, up to the civil rights movement, that's what has defined my reality. People's lives were improved and changed by David Walker, Marcus Garvey, Frederick Douglass, Harriet Tubman, that's my legacy.

Would you say that you're making an excellent, good, fair, or poor living in Ghana now?

In terms of monetary? Well, I mean, I have a good living.

What do you envision the future of Africa to be? It's a large question.

I don't know. It depends on who we decide we're going to be. Because I think Africa, I mean, it has every potential to be strong and independent. It has every potential to just be the marketplace for Europe and America, and their labor force, where a few boys make a little bit of money, and we just keep things rolling so that the average American can live a certain standard of life.

Africa is an enormous continent; there's fifty-four countries there. It's a country with an enormous diaspora which even now is spreading to Europe. You don't watch the world soccer teams. Every country in Europe has an African on its team. Africa is what we decide it will be, who we decide to be culturally.

When you say, "We," you mean?

Africans and the Diaspora. I don't see them as independent.

So what do you envision the future of African-Americans in America?

I think that we're Americans. I mean some people love this place. And they have a right to live here and they have a right to be acknowledged as a body of Americans. But you think a New York Jew feels apologetic about supporting Israel? I mean they may find it complex now. The American Jew will have to add his intelligence to the discourse if what's happening, if Israel is going to survive. They're going to have to make sense between the extremist, the orthodox Jew, and the renewed Jew and this. They're going to have to help Israel define what it's going to be if it's going to survive.

But I think most Jews feel toward Israel like you feel toward a family member. There's things they do that make you crazy, but it's still your family, and push come to shove, you're there. And I'd like to think we could develop that sensibility about Africa, that we would treasure it and find ways to put our heads together so that we can record and articulate.

I mean, look at Ethiopia, one of the greatest, oldest civilizations in this world, and we as some of the most affluent Africans in the world, the African-American, sit here and watch these stupid, exhausting pictures of only starving babies, when there's the oldest Christian church there, there's the oldest Jewish religion there. Everything the Ethiopian does, the incredible monasteries there, and there are churches coming out of the mountainsides, their rugs, the way they clean their meat, the way they prepare coffee, the most delicate rich culture in the world. A monarchy that can trace its lineage back to David. And we're just there talking about, "Oh, isn't that terrible, there are starving kids."

Who the hell cares that in Italy, the lira, you can get a paper bag full of money for twenty dollars. All you see is Michelangelo. What's wrong with us? That's why our kids don't do well in school. That's why you can get a recent immigrant, you look at the recent African immigrants that come here, an Ethiopian, a Ghanaian, a Nigerian, and see how they do in school. It doesn't matter what school they go to, and ask yourself why. It's because our kids have no sense of self. There's no way you can compete with generations of Yankees who feel power, their presence and energy, and you throw your kids in those schools and they're like flies in a bowl of milk. And they're in cultural graveyards for themselves. And the only thing they come out wondering is who they are.

COMMENTS

Although many of the women came to Africa initially as wives to Africans, they quickly developed a clear sense of their role in the new society. Because many possessed college degrees, they were able to find meaningful employment. The most pressing issue was cultural. The relationships between African men and women were quite different from those in the United States. Despite the differences, these women carved out for themselves a satisfying existence.

3

African-American Men Who Returned

Men who came to Africa came for many different reasons. Some were on the run, trying to escape from the draft or from prosecution for political offenses. Some had chosen Africa long before the tumultuous period of the Black Power Movement and, therefore, had established very respectable careers. One physician in Nairobi, for example, had established a practice in tropical medicine that was considered by many to be the best on the West Coast of the continent. They all, however, had a deep affinity for the continent and what it represented.

DARREL OMAR
SEPTEMBER 5, 1972

First question is where were you born?
  I was born in New Orleans, Louisiana.

How long did you live there?
  I was taken from there before I was a year old. My mother was working for the White folks and she went to Maine to work for them while they were on their vacation, and when they got ready to leave and come back to Bickford County, Mom said no, I'm staying here where I'm free, so consequently I was raised and educated in whatever fashion in Portland, Maine, and that's about that.

How long were you in Portland, Maine?
  I graduated from the high school in 1937.

That was Portland High School.
Yes.

Where were you educated and what grade level did you attain?
Grade school, grammar school, and four years of high school, then I sneaked up on a scholarship to go to Howard University for a couple of years. I goofed off, not in the usual sense of goofing off, but I figured I could have a little enjoyment along with my studies as opposed to working plus tutoring as I was. So I went to the Merchant Marines.

How long were you in the Merchant Marines?
For a short while. They got a little thing on me, and I never did get back to Howard University and have no aspirations, although I guess there's nothing wrong with it. I want to clarify that.

Did you continue your education at any point when you got out of the Merchant Marines?
Well, in the academic sense no, but in the factual and real sense yes. Because of the fact that by being in the Merchant Marines I could realize that which heretofore I had been reading about. So therefore it was my consensus of thinking and feeling that my education was really personified when I proceeded to go around the world to see, hear, and do pertaining to living.

Now how many countries did you visit?
Oh man, like I said I've been around the world, once when the war started, I had covered the waterfront.

When did you develop an interest in Africa?
I guess you might say when I first heard of Nkrumah in Ghana, and when I saw for myself that our Black situation in the States wasn't going to materialize to our expectations. Then the only thing I could think of then was to go where I constitute the majority and then perhaps I could receive Black justice as opposed to White justice for Black people. I started to come here in 1960, but I was scared so I left the East Coast and went to the West Coast and stayed there for ten years in California. So in 1970 I got an appropriation from the Boston City Council of sixty-five thousand for the drug program. The people played around and messed around for about three months, and I saw it was a shuck when the money decreased to five thousand, so realizing that for a hundred thousand Black people in Metropolitan Boston. And there is no telling how many of them are junkies. Sixty thousand was a drop in the bucket and was a great big joke. So I decided right then and there before I got scared. I was scared of the language barrier. If there was no communication, then you could not make yourself known or straighten out

anything that was misunderstood. So after thinking to myself that kindness was a universal language and therefore that eliminated that psychological block that had been created in my mind concerning my Black brothers and sisters here in the manner that we had been taught over there. So I decided to come and that was what I did.

You said you started to come in 1960, but you got scared. What did you mean by that?

I guess you could say a few things, but the largest thing was what I just mentioned. The psychological block of the communications barrier. Naturally the thought of giving up all that which you had known and been familiar with all of your life, that was rather shadowing, but not so much for me because I had the previous experience of having been to foreign countries before and that experience led me to believe and know that I was treated anywhere in the world better than I was treated in the United States or any of its territorial possessions or in any country where English was the native dialect. I was treated better in these other countries so therefore it didn't really hold the force of fear of saying just going foreign I managed to convey to myself the thought that in fact I was going home. It was going to be hard, and I would have to earn my way by changing many thoughts, ideas, as well as actions. In the fifteen months that I've been here, it has been rough but factually it hasn't been any rougher than that which I encountered in the United States and I love it.

How old are you and are you married and have any children?

I have two children by a previous marriage and they are grown. I'm fifty-one.

Are any of your children or your wife here?

The wife is here, but the children were by another marriage. I talked with my son just before coming here, and although he is of the younger generation and is pretty hip, I guess the same thing he feels is felt by the younger people. If their foreparents have invested so much, and he too has invested himself because he served in Korea a couple of years. So if he feels that he wants to stay there and continue the fight there then that is his privilege, and he should have the opportunity to execute it and that is the way it is.

Have you met many other Black Americans here who decided to live?

Now you know Bob, I'm going to have to pull you down from on what you just said. I haven't met a Black American in my life.

Well have you met any Afro-Americans or Africans living in America who have decided to live here?

Now we can talk. I just wanted to get the record straight. Yes I have, brother, a few under many different disguises, and I don't think I necessarily need to name them. I have met quite a few and quite a few of them have been tried in terms of their patience and many other areas and factors, but I think on the whole the brothers have the ideas that in terms of fact they can't go back to anything any better than that which they left so that I would risk a hazardous guess and say that anywhere from 25 to 50 percent wouldn't necessarily leave right away, although they became frustrated. They have the tendency to persevere and want to hold out just as I'm doing and as many others have done. I'm familiar with a couple here who are residing here and doing business professionally, and it might suffice to say that the trend now is changing in that the brothers and sisters will either stay here and continue to persevere or they will go to another locale in terms of another free and independent state. That was just about the essence of it, Bob, but as I told you fortunately I've had a little enlightening inspiration, so I think my fight, if I can call it that, might tend to be a little bit easier and perhaps a little more fruitful in the final analysis.

By being in Africa what do you miss about America?

What do I miss most about America? Now I'm not going to play you cheap. I know you are not asking that in the usual sense. At least I'm going to think that, and factually the only thing I can say as a human being that I miss would have to be my family, my mother and father who are fortunately still living. I had to leave them and I'm the only one they've ever had, so the fact that they are old and I had to leave them still in the clutches of pigs, animals, etc., that hurts, and distresses me, but a man does what he has to do. As far as actually missing anything concerning the culture, propaganda, environment, the so-called higher echelon and institutions of academic learning and so forth, I miss none of the falseness, period! Because I see the whole thing as being like Hollywood. So I can't miss anything that's false. I would rather encounter whatever I encounter here because at least it's Black and not being perpetuated upon me because I'm Black. So in terms of fact, brother, I miss nothing in that land except my immediate relatives and some very nice friends. I might say too that there were some pretty good White friends involved, but they were still White. I take it like Malcolm said, I know who my damn enemy is.

Has your conception of America changed as a result of being here?

Has it changed as a result of my residing here during the time I've been here? Very definitely, but not the usual sense. It has changed to the extent that, let me say in the African terminology, a herd of wild elephants couldn't pull me out of here to get me back there. So whatever qualms I had about leaving have only become more reinforced to the extent that I have made up my mind that if and when I die that my blood if it is spilt, and hopefully it won't but if so, it will be spilt on African soil.

What do you do for a living here?

Right now I am waiting to see if I can once again be employed by the government in terms of the area of communications. I was employed, as you know, on the radio, and I think I was the first Black who had a program. First Black African who was born in America, you see. And it's understood that there are always going to be small prejudices, hesitancy concerning new injections or new thinking. So thank God I don't feel overly exasperated with my brothers or a few occurrences that have happened. I just mailed a letter off today to the minister of information in Tanzania, and I have the nerve and audacity to expect a reply. If I had written to the same counterpart office in the States, but, . . . and one other iron I have in the fire here which might tend to allow me to see the man I've come here to see, Mzee himself.

What exactly did you do when you were working for Voice of Kenya and why were you dismissed?

Well, I was doing the program called the sundown from six to eleven and I guess you might say, and you know because you listen to the radio as much as I do, I was the first brother who tended to play and feature music by Black artists who were Africans although they were foreign born. I might add that they have a pretty good library there, and I felt that it would be more beneficial to Black people here in Kenya to realize that musicians and entertainers of their own color were at the highest echelon of professional achievement and I felt it would be a good thing to let the brothers and sisters hear that which was the tops in Black professionalism so that they could only render to you that which was given to me and that is that my English was unintelligible.

That's the only reason they gave?

That is part of the bitter frustration. Yes, that was the only reason they gave, but even so I can compare this to things that have occurred in the streets during my younger years when I was terminated on a job perhaps and wasn't even given that much of a reason or excuse.

I understand there was another African-American who was dismissed along with you. What happened in her case?

Well, I don't make the facts or I have to tell them like they are and it's a matter of record if I can quote verbatim the reason given was the purpose for which she was hired no longer existed and therefore her employment was terminated immediately, but with the ninety days clause of payment for three months. They did honor this concerning myself and the lady. Although it had been a damn bitter pill, Bob. I'm looking at it like this, there had been an injection made in terms of breaking the ice, so who am I to say that perhaps a month or two from now there will come the time when this which has occurred to myself and the lady will not be prominent or pertinent factors, and things will probably be as most of us desire them to be.

Do you find that you've been accepted as a returned brother?

Very definitely! My arm get tired with what they call and people in the States choose to call as the Black power sign. I'm not ashamed of the fact that I say hello by uplifting of my arm in a fist, my right or left arm. I have some people greeting me like that till sometimes the arm gets tired. I consider you as the younger generation, man, and it's up to us who have occupied that seat of the driver to have that communication and understanding with you so that when it's time for me to take a back seat, I don't have to worry because you are going to drive me along in safety and comfort. There has never been no question in my mind concerning acceptance, and I never dwell on that although many people, mostly Caucasian, try to show me as a Black man here concerning my Black brothers and sisters and I'm saying that it is impossible because I know him. Never no question of my being accepted, only a matter of how I carried myself. If I carried myself derogatorily and erroneously then naturally I wouldn't be accepted, just the same as I wouldn't be in any country. No problem with anyone Black who carried themselves in the true African way of kindness, courtesy, and respect, and that is the African way.

Do you find that coming from America is an advantage or a disadvantage?

Now you are really getting down to some nitty-gritty. I think you're testing me personally. Look, factually it's disadvantage, but it's a disadvantage with reservation. It has its advantages as well as disadvantages. In terms of the disadvantages, Bob, this you have to understand and dig deep. Not overly or profusely deep, but you have to get underneath the surface. You see the brother who would not be accepted here in terms of the one who has not vomited himself verbally or action wise, and this is the exhibitancy of nonacceptance. There is a profound reason for that. You see, prior to independence the White government would send a representative from here to America. If he would go into the southern part of America, he would go into a hotel, restaurant, or what have you which had signs stating Black and White. Now the Black brother in the States would see the African, who was born in Africa, come there with his native clothes on and he could walk into this place which said no colored. The brother there would see this man able to do this, and the African born in America who had fought for the country and he cannot go into this place which said no colored. The brother there would see this man able to do this, and the African born in America who has fought for the country, he cannot go into this place where the foreign or native born African can go into. Naturally this caused resentment, that some Caucasians would send an emissary from the States to here, then this brother from the States wearing his native clothes can come here and go into a restaurant or hotel and the brother here sees this man who looks like him and can go into these places and he who was born here and raised here cannot go. This automatically causes a division between the African born in Africa and the African born in America. I think it is fair to say that in later years the tendency has become to overcome that and think for themselves because the Black man there as well as the brother here now knows who sent that Black man here. It's a common enemy, and they realize that this common enemy had been trying to draw a wedge between us and the thinking now has turned to brothers saying to you, we welcome you, we love you, and we want you to stay. They really and sincerely do the best they can. I've eaten in the African homes here and been treated more royally than I've been in some of the richest White homes in America, and I've been in some of the richest.

Do you think you'll go back to the United States or do you plan to stay here? I think you have sort of answered that already.

Hey man, I definitely have, but just to reiterate it in the African terminology. A herd of wild elephants couldn't pull me out of here to get me back there. In other words, I'm saying categorically: Unequivocally, I'm not going back there alive.

Do you speak any African languages?

No, I don't. I'm sure you know that when I was going to school they taught me a couple of foreign languages, but they happened to be French and Latin, and at that time it was not their intention to teach the African in America anything about himself. I might inject at this time that there is so much being discussed at this time of the culture of the so-called Negro race. It is also true that there is no such thing as a Negro. You see scientists have not been able to as yet invent a human being so, therefore, once they did not invent the Black man they cannot name him.

Do you consider yourself political, religious, or artistic?

Now, I'll have to shoot you once again, because of course you can't overcome your culture overnight, but there is no such thing as any of these types of persons. The only kind ... I mean we are all artistic in one way or another but if you want to get into the nitty-gritty of it, I'm a human being and my race is the human race and my tribe is Black and that's where it is. None of these superficial labels and so forth, which that culture we were both born into tends to label individuals with. I am first a human being, and my race is the human race. And I won't conduct myself as a human being that will allow you or anybody else to categorize me in whatever category your opinion leads you to assume that I'm in. Now from talking to me that few times that you have I would prefer for you to answer that. I've given in fact I had to take a few interviews even when I was going this program we have to turn around, and I don't think of it as an interview in the usual eyes in the States. I think of it as a small amount of time in which two individuals will get together and discuss, and hopefully from their discussion will emanate that which will be equally beneficial to not only those two participants, but to those who might have the opportunity to listen to that conversation after.

Why did you leave America?

I know you know why, but you just want me to verbalize it. Huh. Well, let me get a little deep on that. In the first place, it was not my home. My ancestors were taken from another land there against their will, and none of their descendants were ever given the privilege or opportunity to ascertain as to whether or not they wanted to stay or to be taken to the land their ancestors came from. Citizenship was forced on my ancestors, and they could only live from hand to mouth and could never have the privilege of traveling. And after seeing the demonstrations and I choose to call them rebellions as opposed to riots, after seeing, hearing, and dealing with the so-called liberals, left wings, right wings, communist, democrats, and republicans and the whole thing I came to the final conclusion that I don't know what a communist is and that's suppose to be the biggest threat on the country. I don't know what a democrat and a republican is. Neither one of them means this damn Black man any good, so therefore I decided that if I must lose them at least I'm going to do it where I had an opportunity to win. The only way I have an opportunity to win is to first constitute the majority. Here in this land my blackness constitutes the majority, and that's why I left there.

The current thought in the United States among Black political leaders is that the Blacks should become more integrated into the political structure by electing more mayors, congressmen, and through the political system they can bring themselves up. Do you share that belief at all?

I definitely do not. How can you possibly attain or acquire that which you have the so-called democratic right to when in all of the precepts and concepts in the States, whether written at this time, we are their inferiors. If you look back upon the highest decision-making body in the land in terms of justice, you will find that the Supreme Court of the United States actually delivered a decision to the effect that the Black man was a chattel and therefore had no rights as a human being. Through the years this kind of thing has changed, but it is only changed on paper and not changed in terms of actuality. Therefore you couldn't possibly win. The only person they could get to, in my opinion, is to Judas who will accept the thirty pieces of silver. Frankly, I'd like to state that I think that Mayor Hatcher and Carl Stokes are actually not bought, and even if they are, every man has to do his thing his way. If he doesn't do it in the way that pleases the majority or should I say the majority of people concerned, then eventually there will tend to be some kind of elimination. How this will take place is not for me to say. Man might die like Reverend M. L. King died. It might even be a honky that will take that man out because of whatever. So there is no possible way where you are outnumbered in terms of at least fifteen to one. No possible way for the Black to acquire political freedom or political justice. It's impossible.

I think the Panthers would agree with you in that it is impossible to get justice there, but at the same time they would wage a revolution on the continent itself. How do you feel about that?

Bob, it's a funny thing. I just left the Black doctor who is staying here, and as you see this article there that I'm reading is old. I think this is dated February 23, 1971. I didn't come here until September 1971, "The Panthers and The Law," I feel so that I want to get back into a little taste. Those brothers got more guts then I have, man. They are fighting a losing battle. Every Black man, woman, and child in the past who has fought for justice; everyone at the present and all in the future who are fighting for justice, not Black justice not White justice, or green, people, or whatever. But justice in the actual sense of the word. Those people, and it's a damn shame to say it but they've died for nothing. But the pitiful part about it, all those who will die in the future, they will die for nothing because there will be no damn justice for them. So if the Panthers want to commit to that, then honestly I'm saying more power to them, good luck, God love 'em, and God bless them. And for every one of them that gets offended and I'm reading in where, you know it's a honky right of course, he said the people were at first afraid of the Panthers, as a menace, and then later when the Panthers seemed to have been getting the worse end of the deal, that's a psychological thing. You see, the Panthers were getting the worse end of the deal, that's the psychological thing. You see the Panthers were getting the worse end of the deal from the beginning, not that they were oppressing others and then when a few of them got killed, now just is now being, you know retribution and all that. I'm saying they were hassled and hurt from the beginning, and then the pig just showed its true colors. He up and decided that they, who want justice, were committing a cardinal sin and a cardinal crime. When have you ever seen in the courts of the United States of America a man bound and gagged with a hood placed over him, over his head, all because he is saying what the Constitution gives you a right to. He has a right to defend himself and he has a right to face his accusers. And he was tried by his peers. Well, there's no White man who can be a Black man's peer. So, therefore, the whole thing is a great big farce, and the pig is only showing his true colors. I'll go on record as saying, you're damn right my name used to be Nelson, but it's Darrel Omar now, and there is no way between heaven and hell that a honky will ever make me bend, bow, or whatever. You will not kill me by low economic torture or whatever. You will kill me quickly and mercifully. 'Cause if I'm gonna die, I'm damn sure gonna try to take him with me. Even Steven, and when he knows that if he pulls his pistol I'm pulling mine, we gonna shoot together, now he will want to commit to some dialogue, and at that time when we face each other over the end of a barrel too then I am willing to dialogue. But that is the condition under which I am willing to dialogue because if he doesn't have his weapon out of my face where I can see it, then if we are sitting at a table as we are now, I have no doubt whatsoever that he got it pointed right at a table as we are now. I have no doubt whatsoever that he got it pointed right dead at my gut. But he doesn't know that Black man is awake now. Malcolm woke everybody. He didn't hide behind the collar of ministry, whatever, messenger and God, and all like that. He was a man and he just said Black man, get up off your knees and when you get up off your knees you stand up tall. You know and the kinks and stiffness has gone out of your joints; you feel good and you're not in too much of a damn hurry to bend back down there again because it's kind of hard on your knees and when you get off your knees you stand up and tell him. Now you got everything to lose but I ain't got a damn thing to lose. You got your trust fund paid up, your endowments, your insurance. You got the two-car garage with the two cars. You got the twenty, thirty thousand dollar Colonial. You got everything to lose. You got your wardrobe, your twenty or thirty thousand dollar a year job. And you got your wife and all the equipment in the house, so you have everything to lose. I have nothing to lose, so when you come messing with me you damn sure stand a chance of losing it cause I ain't playing.

What are your feelings on the Nation of Islam? Elijah Mohammed program?

Well, I most of the time refuse to talk about what I don't know. But I think

I can give you an honest opinion. I have different times visited the Mosque. I saw nothing wrong with the orderly or sergeant at arms, or whatever you choose to call him. I saw nothing wrong with him asking you, or me rather, to take all my possessions out of my pocket and put them into an envelope, and he'd write my name on it and he put it in a slot for me. I didn't hear anyone in there preaching "kill whitey." I heard him preaching don't associate with him, period. And I agree with this wholeheartedly and completely. The best way to deal with him is don't, and then you don't have to worry about him double-crossing, distrusting, or anything like that. I think personally that the Nation of Islam definitely could stand improvements, but I am not speaking of it negatively for the simple reason that what facility or organization in existence today cannot stand improvement? So therefore I'm not gonna allow the blame to be placed on the Nation of Islam. I don't know that they have helped many needy people. I don't know that the media tends to distort, and it tends to play to the weaker minds of the Black brothers and sisters there. Well, thank God most of them are cognizant that their lot is as hard to bear as it could possibly be and that therefore they are exhibiting freedom of execution in terms of getting together. Very contrary to that which a lot of people try to convey, I, during the three times that I've been in the temple, the mosque, the particular one in Boston, on Intervale Street, I have never, at any time, heard them preach the so-called radicalism. But if one Black would say to another Black, let's get together and combine our strength, let's get together and do that which is beneficial for us Blacks, immediately the Caucasian media will turn around and designate that particular endeavor as radical and Black—Black in terms of dirty, violent, and filthy. But I'd also like to inject here at this time. You know, it is funny that each and every year the Caucasian spends billions in oils and cosmetics and so forth, not only under God's own sun, but equally under what they call ultraviolet rays and all that, trying to get Black just like me. I'd elucidate you to something else at this time, too. The honky Bible has put the honky's business in the streets, but it's the most ignored piece of literature that was ever written. The honky Bible tells everybody of every color just what the honky is. The honky had told you that God is Black, even with that he holds most sacred. But you will never hear any of his ministers, preachers, pastors, or whatever he was asked the question of whether he would want his daughter to marry a Black man. He said "no," and he gave his validation that the children would suffer. Well, I say like this no damn body told Billy Graham who the hell to marry. And if he is for real in the ministry of God, if he sees things going contrary to that which God designated, then it's his duty, but you know he wants to play games, so they got a lot of 'em. Where was I on that again?

The Bible said that God was Black?

Oh yes, dig this, man. It say in there that of dust thou art to dust thou shall return, OK. He said he made you in his own image. Well, if you have ever seen white dust. The whitest White man in the world. What we call in terminology state-side albinos. When he dies he turns blacker than you and I. This is proof positive that man was made from the dust of the earth, that dust of the earth got to be black then. Now if God said he made man in his own image and he made him out of some black dust, then what color is God? Do you see my point? Well, he also told them they want to play games about the Jew being the chosen people. You remember our first conversation when I elucidated you to this. It says in the Bible that Jesus Christ was a Jew. It also said in that honky Bible that Jesus Christ had hair like lamb's wool. Well, baby, lamb's wool is just like you and my hair. I haven't seen a whole lot of sheep or lamb's wool or none of that, but I've seen enough to know that. So therefore, that contradiction, that thing of the pictures that he shows of Christ, you know, in terms of his hair long, flowing, and silken. You see what I'm trying to say. Further clarification for that is the fact that the first man that God chose to give the Ten Commandments to, it says in the Bible verbatim, Moses black but comely. The wisest man in the world, in the Bible was said to be Solomon was who Black. But in recent years during your mother and father's time as well as mine it's changed. The revised, what they call the King James version, well this tends to take away from the black, and they gonna have Solomon's color be darkened, swarthy. All these kinds of jokes, man, this is just indications of what he's been doing all the time.

Do you think that African consciousness on the part of Afro-Americans is a helpful experience?

Do you think that African consciousness on the part of that African who was born in America, you mean? Say, man, let me put it like this, the first thing they want to say to him is forget your color. How the hell can I forget it if he won't forget it. Now I feel that we Black folk automatically have that kind of consciousness because we don't resort to and inject the kind of actions that the Caucasian injects. He sometimes tends to think that we are ashamed of our blackness. Now there have been periods and interludes when, shall we say about the conking of the hair, I used to do it. It wasn't the case of well I shall be ashamed of my blackness, but rather it was a case of I would be treated, perhaps, hopefully that is, less as a nigger if I had the straight hair which was continually being pushed at me through their media, in terms of newspaper, radio, television, magazines, etc. And I think it's fair to say we know we could never be anything but Black, even the person of a fairer pigmentation who is White in his actual color but whose past grandfather of grandmother was Black. Even this person he knows that his parents or relatives were raped and that therefore he is Black, and he does not want to be a part of that which was raped, in fact, his mother or his grandmother. So it's definitely a beneficial thing but it's not that, that is something that could not even be put to question. You see take yourself, for instance, if you were not aware of that blackness, and if you did not feel proud and good because of that blackness, then you would not be here on the Black continent, so-called Black, but it's Black and stone-cold beautiful. Ain't that where it's at, brother?

Do you think that a substantial number of Black Americans should come to Africa and settle?

There you go again with that word Black American. Hey, brother it's all right, all right. I mean that from the heart. You can't come out of that bag overnight, that's not derogatory. Sometimes I turn around and refer to myself as Omar Nelson, so it's no shame as long as you know what the hell you mean. The time will come when your words will automatically assert that which you mean. The time will come when your words will automatically assert that which you mean in terms of that blackness. You have to forgive me for deviating. What was that again brother? Well, let's put it like this. Malcolm fell out with someone I guess you might say when his ideas became a little too radical. But he did state chickens come home to roost. So that's my answer.

Do you feel like an African, Afro-American, or American?

OK. I'm going to give you a little rundown. This is fact. First of all let's take it factually. The White American is white, and therefore to me there is only one American. That's him. He did not invent the Indian so he cannot call him an American, because that Indian is an Indian. Now that Indian was possessor of the land, earth, and so therefore the invading American cannot give him citizenship now. In terms of fact, you look at the African here, his hair is curly like mine. My ancestors came from here factually against their will, they have never applied for citizenship. I didn't either, my parents neither, and neither did any of my foreparents. So therefore in terms of fact, and in terms of legality I am not an American. So naturally I think for their own perseverance, for own human dignity, they must come there to that place where there are others like them and where their pigmentations are not derogatory. No one condescends to treat them as human. No one will render derogatory decisions such as you're a chattel, you have no human rights. You are in fact a subhuman. You see, most people don't realize it but the White man has tribes, too. You take the Germans, the Danes, Norwegians, the Belgians, the Swedish, the Austrians, Czechoslovakians, Yugoslavians—they all have one thing in common. They are all White, but they all speak different languages. So believe me that is proof, positive proof, they too are different tribes, just like the tribes here in Africa.

Some Black Americans have traveled internationally and have stated that Europeans are quite different from White Americans. Has that been your impression from your travels around the world?

Bob, very definitely. You remember at the first part of the interview I told you that I was treated better in Europe. Europe seems to be more free. But I never told you that I was treated better in Europe. Europe seems to be more free. But I never allowed that now to disillusion me. I'm stating categorically, the White man is afraid of the Black man, and therefore he has to fear him. Now I can't answer as to why he fears him, you have to ask him and I doubt very seriously as to whether he would elucidate you in terms of truth. They have to get a Kinsey report to validate their virility and all like that. He, like Eldridge Cleaver said, the Black man is a supermasculine menial. When he begins to think for himself, be becomes a threat to the omnipotent administrator, the White man. He just wants to involve himself in thinking and delivering directives. The supermasculine Black man is just suppose to do without thinking. Now if he begins to think then he'll climb upon that plane and level that will become precariously unbalanced. The White man cannot afford to let that Black man up on that level because it will tilt it, and all of them will come sliding off back down here into this jungle. But we're all in a jungle, and thank God the thing I have in my mind here is that under this man here. He's the only leader in the world who's been to jail for his people. That's Mzee Jomo Kenyatta. This man had done something here that the United Nations can view with pride and shame because they have been so negligent. This man has seen to it that his government and his people get along together. You find the policemen walking here without pistols, without blackjacks, without nightsticks, without locks, handcuffs. No shotguns, dogs, riot equipment, all that stuff. They respect law here. The African culture is truly coming out here.

What do you envision the future of Africans living in America to be?

In one word: HELL!

CLARENCE EDWIN
AUGUST 3, 1972

Why did you come to Africa?

My daughter is here, who to me represents the next generation coming. That's the important thing. My only purpose is to be here and earn just a reasonable livelihood. And I'm here to assist basically in that. And toward that end I'm dedicated and toward that end I'm giving myself. And therefore I feel that I belong here, and by no other circumstances could I be reached as an expatriate in that sense. I originally am from West Virginia. I was born there in the coal field district in a little place nobody knows. Inducted into the service from there and came back to college at the local college, Bluefield State, and from there I went to Philadelphia to a technology school there which is still there, Franklin School of Technology. From there I went to California and I been there since. So since 1943 I have been in California, Los Angeles, till I came here in 1966.

What is your educational background?

I have a bachelor's in technology from the Institute of Philadelphia, Franklin School of Science and Arts. And my professional degree is D.C. I'm a doctor of chiropractic that was attained from Los Angeles College of Chiropractors of California.

What exactly are chiropractors?

It is a form of medical practice. But we don't use surgery, that is, we are not trained in surgery. But it is otherwise the entire field of therapeutics, minor surgery. We just don't do surgery.

When did you develop an interest in Africa?

Oh, that has been all the time. I was taught that by my father. That was no development. That was part of our education that our father gave us in those days when of course it wasn't taught in the public schools. At the time when we did get a chance to go to public schools because that was not always so where I came from. But my father taught me and that has been with us all the time.

I find that interesting because a lot of old people, the older generation, they don't have much interest in Africa, yet your father did?

For instance, he would sit and talk to us often. My father was an interesting man. He would sit and talk. He visualized Africa as our homeland. He would often tell us that, and strange enough you see those things stuck with us. Now if you take a small child and keep telling him that same thing and you are his father he believes you. He hears you and the remnants are forever there. So he taught us because days were dark then in the southern counties of West Virginia; days were dark for Black people. So he was telling us soon, he said you want to grow up you get an education, you go to Africa because you don't belong here. He said that from the time I know. The books, he purchased, which I have. Any number of them, I have the books he purchased for us when we were growing up. They all Negro history books. The Carter Garland Woodson was powerful in those days and a Du Bois, well, he bought all those books and he would read from those to us. And as a result we were taught an awareness of this as our home.

How large is your family?
    Seven.

Have they sort of wandered back to Africa?
    No, they are still in the States. We are in contact, but they are still in the States.

Why do you think that out of the seven children, you are the one who took your father's advice and came back to Africa?
    I think they believed it and all, but they don't want to take the risk. Some people concerned about security and so forth and so on. If I based my move on security, I would have been in California right now. If I had based my move on that and that alone. That is, my security and the way I was living, and where I was living, and the years and time that had been put in and the money, such little as was accumulated. If I were looking at it from that viewpoint, I would still be there. They are just reluctant to make the changes.

Was your father's father a slave?
    Yes, oh yes.

If this is not too personal, how old are you?
    I'm fifty-five.

And are you married?
    Yes, my wife is in America. She has been there since. She came to stay here six months. She's back in the hospital, she has psychiatric problems.

How many children do you have?
    One.

And is she with you now?
    Yes. She's in Mombasa.

How long had she been in Africa?
    She was here before I was.

And is she planning on staying, too?
Oh yes, she's a citizen.

Have you met many other Black Americans who have decided to live in Africa?
No. I met one in Tanzania.

By being in Africa, do you miss anything about America?
Yes, it's prejudice. Tense psychological feelings that I had ever with me that I don't have here. The feeling that when I go down to check on a matter or look into something and always felt I got the raw end of the stick so to speak. While here they may be slow, but whatever I'm entitled to I will get it. It may be next year and I'm suppose to get it this year, but I will get it. It's just their way of doing things. They don't deliberately try to take from me anything—that I can say so far. Whatever I was due here as a person I have found that I will get it. It's just that they don't move like you Americans with swiftness and correctness at the moment. He tells you to come Monday and you come Monday, then he'll tell you another day, any other day you see, but you'll get it.

Did you suffer any overt act of discrimination when you were living in the United States?
Of course, those things I didn't think they needed any speaking of because they are so factual until it is redundant just for me to go into that. In West Virginia where I was born and even coming to California, but certainly in West Virginia in those days, you can imagine what was happening to us. Then certainly that old back of the bus stuff. Negroes and Whites do not go to school together. That was then in the state constitution, where that state university you could not attend. Even after I came to California, you find the same thing. It's just more subtle in another manner. But it's the same thing.

What kind of work are you doing here?
Research technologist in biochemistry.

How long have you been working there?
I just began there the first of April this year. Prior to that time I was two years at Coast General Hospital. And two years there at the Kenyatta Hospital. I was transferred then to the Coast in Mombasa. The Coast General Hospital which is a hospital similar to the Kenyatta, serving the coast in the same capacity.

Was it difficult finding employment here?
Well you see, everything I've done, I've done on my own so to speak, without any channels. So I tried to make my intercession before I came. And I was told that nothing could be done unless I reported in person here. They

said if you are willing to report in person then I'll be assured of someplace. Then I was not sure of what it would be, but it would be a placement in the field similar to what I was working in, depending upon where they needed me the most. He had told me already, when I say he, I'm referring to the director of medical services, that they could not give me rights to practice here in the beginning. He said but you can come like you say you want to. I wrote him a letter and explained why I didn't attempt to channel through an official channel, that I was doing it on my own and I was interested from that aspect and I told him why. And he said we can always use one of such training, yet you are willing to take a job asking lesser than what your experience, qualifications will entitle you to. Well, that to me is still secondary. So I told him yes and took it at that upon face value and I came.

So you have been in Kenya for how long?
Since July, five years now or a little better now, since '66.

So have you applied for citizenship yet?
I have, but I don't know about it yet.

Is it very hard to get citizenship?
Yes.

Why is that? If you have a profession like yours?
That doesn't matter, you see that they think that we think sometimes. As I write to my people back home and tell them, when I mention certain things, I say if it seems odd to you, it sounds like it might not be true, don't doubt it. Just accept it because I am telling it to you. It is what I have found as living on the ground here and not reading it out of a book. So it sounds odd sometimes and maybe it isn't what you have read in official documents there, but it's the way it is when you get here. So it doesn't matter if various other things intercede between that. Surely they would need many people of the kind that doesn't mean you going to accept them either. First in many cases the setup is arranged in such a manner that the ex-colonial lords would rather not see some people get in here, you know. And therefore, they will do as they have done in our case, and say here you have man, he goes to the university and gets a Ph.D. in chemistry. They don't give him a job, but just living quarters. I don't believe that people just give away things. America didn't get to her state of advancement economically and otherwise technologically as she is now by giving away. So if she gives anything she sees what she's getting or intends to get in return. But Blacks have received very little support or very little recognition in that manner because they didn't understand what was happening here. That qualifications. Good, he does, and yet they need him but they

don't need him. And why? Because the Danish, the Swedish, the British, and the American will always send in men and they pay for him. So you who would need to come in and you would expect remuneration on the basis of the salary they are supposed to allocate. Then you find that you are not taken. And the reason you are not taken is that they are gonna get your equivalent, supposedly for nothing. I don't think it's ever for nothing. So therefore you are left out.

You think that is the case mainly in Kenya?

No, it's all over. It's a part of the strategy. You see, through the United Nations many of the bodies and quasi-governmental organizations connected therewith, that's the method—to help this continual employment of their own people in Africa here. To me it is still a very subtle plan. I view it as a subtle plan to keep you from advancing because you see, they're gonna tell you yes. Here you go out to the university. Now when you trace why you will find that supposedly it isn't costing the university any money. So to me that keeps you ever subjugated in the most important place: where you want intellectual development. They keep you subordinated there because you don't get your own in there in the first place. They remain in there and they claim they are helping you but it's not costing you any money.

Have you known this to happen to other Black Americans? They applied and just didn't get citizenship for any obvious reasons?

They applied. You see those who came in, the few that came in the earlier times like my daughter, who took it immediately because she had married and it was automatic at the time. If you applied for it, you had to come and apply. Well, when she married this man here in Kenya she applied the same time. She did and she got it, but that is the only one. Now to apply now, I know two besides myself that have applied and they have gotten the same sort of treatment. But you see you have to be here five years before you could apply. And things have gotten so strange in that manner till there's a great deal of confusion in terms of this immigration. But not many Blacks, as far as I know, apply because most of them come and don't come apparently to remain.

What do you like best about Africa?

Oh, I think for me I like the scenery and the opportunities. The fairness, too. I know that this harkens back to the South, the fairness with which I'm treated. That's all, that will answer everything. The fairness with which I'm treated and that is the finest thing I like about it.

Do you think that you have been accepted as a returned brother?

No, I don't think that I have in that sense. Nor have I felt that I have a de-

sire to propel that sort of image, because I know that culturally I am at vari-
ance. Quite a bit. So I realize that and it is one of the mistakes of geography
or history, or something. . . . Or maybe it wasn't a mistake. But anyway it's a
fact of geography and history so I don't try to become a part of something
that I don't really feel I'm a part of, that's all. Just like the White man, I don't
feel that I'm a part of his structure, and I deal with it because I must deal
with it as a matter of business and survival. But to go out of my way to try to
become accepted by him—no, never, ever, here nor there. The same here, I
realize there's no problem. I don't feel the same as I do when I have to go to a
setup where there's a lot of the White boys. I don't feel the same. I never try
to make this overt effort that I'm trying to be a brother. I just go along and try
to do the best I can. I'm with them constantly but I never try to get over in
their deeper matters because I know I can't understand and then their tribal
ways you see like certain things if I let myself go I will act as though I act in
the normal situation, which is normal to me for where I come. There is no
way yet that I can wipe that out. For example, when I say that I mean this.
You go out sometimes. You go away. You go to a place, and the women will
sit this side of the wall and the men sit here. These little decorums of that
sort where you're used to talking freely. Well, there is a little difference.
Therefore I rather I don't become an absolute socialist because of that. I'll
go whenever it's a mandatory thing because I don't do much socialization.
But if I must go, I will go. And then I'm just observing and take a low key.

*Some of the African students who I have come upon complain that the Afro-
American students stick together too much. Do you think that is bad?*
   Well, I think the reason for that is after all so many of them are in official
capacity here, and I can understand that many of them do represent to the
African an expatriate. He represents to him the same as the White
man—only he's just a dark man. Because they represent some phase of offi-
cialdom. If he goes out, he goes out representing USAID on some project
out there. So they look at him the same way that they do the colonial expatriate. The ones here are on official business, most of them are on official business. I grant that he doesn't become too allied in a way with them. I'm not
here on official business. I'm here on my own. Because my daughter got
around quite a bit. She mingles far more than anybody else I know because
her ideas would allow her to do that, where I wouldn't want to. She likes to
go up-country. Well, the way they live up in some of those places and things,
I don't want to go, unless I had to go. God knows ain't no use saying I would.
I wouldn't want to go and live under the circumstances they have to live under, while she does, she voluntarily does it.

Do you think that coming from America has been an advantage or a disadvantage here as far as how you were accepted by the African?

No, I think it is a help and not a hindrance. Because there is a certain degree of respect for American technology here, for American financial success. So I have profited although I am antisystem, I guess.

Do you speak any African languages?

No, I just speak kitchen Swahili. That allows me to get along here.

Do you consider yourself a political, religious, or artistic person?

I have no specific religion. I do consider myself constantly viewing political situations because the help determines our destiny, as I see it. So, therefore, I must be concerned with it even when I'm not in a position to participate. I'm fully aware.

And what about artistic?

Well, I'm a scientist by training, professional. I'm a scientist.

Why did you leave America?

I left America because I was fed up. This didn't happen on the spur of the moment. This has been a thing that I've been trying to get enough money to do for a long, long time. And I never did get enough money. But finally circumstances such as the Watts riots in which I was, gave me just enough spark to say "finished." Regardless of what I lose, that's it. It was time to go. I felt it was my time to go.

What particularly about Watts?

It wasn't anything about Watts. It was the surrounding circumstances, not the place where I was. No, I couldn't say I wanted to leave there. But some things like that just happened in sufficient order to give us the spark to go ahead then. Irregardless of what, so that was all that was needed. Just some difficulties of that sort because some of us were in that before the riots erupted. There were many undercurrents long before the eruption to the surface. So, we were in this before this great eruption took place. We know how the thing was. For example, where I was in practice at the time and we were approached and coerced in a manner to support certain political candidates who happened not to have been our men—merely because they had been there for a quarter of a century, and he had been exploiting the people. Well, a few of us come along the scene and we are determined to do something about it, then we run into the great power structure. And that's what I encountered. I was told beforehand as some brothers right now whose name I can give in Los Angeles right now. They had to stop being president of NAACP. He had to get out to certain organizations, because he was a dentist by profession. He had been given the word, you are too active. That's why I said that as long as I'm alive I'm concerned with political situations. The politicians giveth and he taketh your right to do this. And so they have the same right to take it away. You wonder why you never see some of us taking an active part. Many of them do take an active part under the scene. But because they will come to you as they did to some of us, some of us didn't hear as I didn't and was given an unduly bad time. Because I refused to hear.

What bad things did they do to you?

I just wanted that little community where I was practicing. It was a ghetto as they say. But I loved the ghetto. It was my place. I'm a ghetto man. If you call it that. It's my home and I understand it so it's all right with me. So I was there, now since I viewed it this way I'm coming in from the South where we didn't have opportunities and so forth. I see these wide open opportunities here. I say, what are you people doing? Right here on the corner here you are. If it isn't ten million dollars that passes here a year, not one dollar and not one single penny of it goes into your hands. They ever employ a Black person? Never. Not until I came and began to put some pressure, that kind of pressure. So then the word begins to get around, who is this troublemaker in this community. I began to say what's wrong you fellas don't fix this place up on Christmas holidays like you do the others. I'm willing to do so and so why can't we do it. They said you are out of your mind. That's what these White merchants tell me. I spent my own money. I was putting much money, $2,000 one time, to beautify the little area. They wouldn't put one thin penny, so we started like that. So you see I don't hear their arguments. When that happened this man running for assembly from that area, now they had gerrymandered the district. See, I didn't want to go into those things, it's a terrible thing. It's the same type of old thing they have always done. First none of us lived over there across the tracks. But here this man had just gerrymandered a small area so that is supposedly where he lived. That constituted an area of ours. Yet 97 percent of these people were Black, and of course we knew who he was that represented the area. So when time for election commenced, of course and who was getting these meetings and trying to influence the people. Look at our state in life. Look at ourselves. What are we doing? Millions of dollars pass through here and you are the poor downtrodden. Why? We did something. For an example, we won a black minister for that post and he succeeded.

Which post was that?

This was an assemblyman post. But this assemblyman who we knew was really pushing it because he knew how these people had been for the past twenty-five years. And so he wants to know who is this? Who is this group behind these people that's beginning to prod him and push him. When he finally found out, they began to come directly or send first their emissaries. They couldn't do that, then finally this particular individual came directly. And you were told then that this support is needed. And I say to the man that after all I am of these people and I earn my living here in this community. And I cannot violate the wishes of the comunity in regards to that. And he said but the wishes of the community has been with me for twenty-five years. I said but the wishes aren't with you now. And he didn't buy that. He said you know you are doing alright and you have much to lose. So these are some of the things you see, and you know what it means when they tell you that. You have much to lose. You have your practice rights in this state. You have your office, everything lined up. You're doing alright. That's to threaten you. He is saying that I can break you, I can break you down. So some of us didn't. I, for one, didn't. We discussed it. I did with my wife before, and she said you do what you think you can live with. That's because money wouldn't mean anything to me if I had to get it that way, then I just couldn't accept it. So I said no, I told him that I would let him know in a few days and I did. I told him frankly that I couldn't do it. He said well you know these things become very difficult. I said I know I'm prepared to take whatever I have to take. I'll fight as long as I can, then when I can't, I'll take whatever I have to take. So I fought him in every way, and of course our man was elected and I began to have trouble, trouble you better know it. So you see I have pulled three years in the penitentiary there in California, so that's how I know what this girl is going through. I understand and it was all for this. Just this, because you are a maverick, you are really. Now these are things that you don't read in books. But it is known to people in the community, they know. Now the point is that you could fine me on nothing for what I did but they'll fine you on other reasons. That's why he come to tell you that it can be difficult. In other words, the district attorney, and so on, after all these people are in the power cahoots. Really if I'm the district attorney and so my brother is the judge, so to speak how easy? We can set any kind of charge. It's for you to disprove it. Despite they say it's the way round but we know it's not. When you have charged me with something. I know if it's a Black man, I know it's predominantly up to me to disprove that, if I can. And so the next thing I know they are giving us a bad time, a real bad time.

You had to spend three years in the penitentiary. What charges did they have against you?

You see he gets where it hurt most. He came to me again and said you had better change your mind and help us. I told him no, just like that. I said there

is no need for further talk. I had a good lucrative practice. Where do you
think they try to hurt you the most? He couldn't come and say I wouldn't
support him in the campaign. I'm not worried about that, he begins to dis-
turb your practice. They come searching your place. They want to find
dope. They can harass you. They became that way. So that didn't work. I felt
it all right but it didn't. It only helped me in the eyes of my people who knew
me. They knew why they were doing it. So that didn't harm me at all. It was
just a nuisance, and it was quite a disturbance. It was embarrassing and hu-
miliating. But it did not hurt me financially, it only helped me. So then they
came around to find something for malpractice.

The current trend is . . .

I have very little faith in the system existing in America so far as justice is
concerned and right. I have little faith in that. I don't think that's gonna
come to us until we ourselves have our own. I just can't see how.

STAN WEBSTER
OCTOBER 2, 1971

Oh, you don't want my name first? [Stan Webster.]

Where were you educated and how much did you have?

I went to public schools in Baltimore and got a bachelor's of architecture
from Howard University, Washington.

When did you develop an interest in Africa?

Oh, I grew up with an interest in Africa. My mother was very pro-Africa
from the time we were kids. So I always had a bit of interest in Africa.

How large a family do you come from?

There were ten children and a half dozen extras all the time. I was a real
depressed kid.

What do you mean the extras?

Oh, people used to leave kids with us for six months, eight months. One
cousin lived with us for seven years. Couple other cousins grew up with us.
It was always a big house, big house, big family.

How old are you? And are you married and have children?

Yes, I'm forty-one, married, and have one child, five years old.

And are they with you in Africa?

Yes, the child was born here.

Have you met many other Black Americans who have decided to spend a great deal of time in Africa?

Oh yes, I've met quite a number. Most of them here have decided to stay. Those residing here, I think I've met most, but it's not a large number however.

About how many would you say approximately?

Oh, about a dozen.

By being in Africa what do you miss most about America?

Well, being in Nairobi, I miss the department stores more than anything else. When you go to shop you have to run around to all these little shops to buy this, that, and the other. Rather than going into one department store and it's all laid out. That's probably the biggest thing that I miss.

A lot of Black Americans I talk to say they miss soul music and dancing. Do you miss that at all?

No, that doesn't bother me.

I guess you're sort of beyond that state, being middle aged.

I don't think middle age. But anyway I got some music I brought with me and things, but I'm not too much into soul. For I've got gospel music, that's as pure soul as you can get. Soul is just a takeoff from gospel, and I got a lot of gospel at home . . .

Has your conception of America changed as a result of being in Africa?

Yes, it has because actually I sort of appreciated a lot of the things that America has done more that I did when I was in the States. When you see what other countries have done, you see that America has done a lot more than other countries in helping Africa along. You don't see this in the States, but when you get here. For instance, with the French, how little the French have done and how all the other countries are exploiting as much as they can, you begin to appreciate and get a different picture of what America is doing. I'm not whitewashing America by any means, but comparatively, they have done a lot more.

Is that the only way your conceptions have changed about it?

Yes, I think basically that's the only way. When you are a ways from something, the bad points sort of tend to mellow a little bit. So this is to be expected.

How long have you been here?

I've been here for seven years.

Are you a citizen yet?
No, I'm not a citizen.

Are you going to apply for citizenship?
Well, I don't know, but I haven't.

Did you meet your wife here?
No, I met her in New York.

What do you like best about Africa and Kenya in particular?
I like the fact that I'm able to do something meaningful here which I would never be able to do in the States. The work that I'm doing is a contribution. It's building up the country, as opposed to in the States where it's a matter of sitting down, holding a job, or tearing down one building and putting up another. Actually you are doing something. I designed the medical school, I mean free clinical medical school. Well, it's pretty much completely my own effort because I had to search out what was needed and how to set it up and so forth. And now the free clinical section is running on what I set up. You have a definite influence.

You're saying that in America these opportunities just don't exist for Blacks?
Not for me, it doesn't.

For you or Black people in general?
I think for Black people generally it doesn't. The one or two that it does is so small and meaningless. And the things you are so completely lost in the great mass that it really has no effect. You can write a letter here in answer to the government criticizing something, and you can find that the whole system will be changed from the result of something that you have come up with. If it's a pretty good idea and you have a pretty receptive person, you can really make a point.

What do you do for a living here?
I'm an architect.

And you own your own office?
Yes, I have my own office.

And how many people do you employ?
Three, and a part-time typist.

How many Black architects would you say there are in Kenya?
One other than myself.

So you are the second one?

I'm second. There is one Kenyan and myself.

Do you think that you get a fair share of the business around here?

Yes, I think I do. In fact I think I get more. I can get as much work as I can handle. But I must say that not one set of my work is from a White American or a White American company.

Why do you think that is?

Because they are White Americans, and they don't change their colors 'cause they leave or change their spots because they leave the States.

So most of your clientele has been from what countries?

Kenyans and Europeans, but no Americans. I'm doing some work for some Black Americans but no White ones.

What kind of work is that?

I'm doing housing, factory. You mean for the Black Americans? Well factory, publishing house, and housing projects, large housing projects.

Are these Black Americans who have become citizens here or are they just opening up businesses here?

One has become a citizen and the other is just an entrepreneur doing development.

Do you find that you have been accepted as a returned brother?

Yes, I think in general. There is very much acceptance for Black Americans here. You find an awful lot of it, especially the people I deal with. I find that they have gone to school in the States. These are Kenyans, and you have a sort of affinity with them. They appreciate you.

So would you say that most of your friends are Kenyans, or do you hang around with many Black Americans?

I don't hang out with anybody much. But I completely have over a whole range, Kenyans, Americans, Europeans, and some Asians.

The reason I asked is that my experience is that when Black Americans come they tend to stick together a lot, and I just wondered if that was the case with you? If many blacks came here do you think that they should stick together as much as they do?

No, I don't think it is a good idea to stick together as much as they do. But you shouldn't force yourselves apart. I have met people here who just tried to be Africans, and they're not Africans. And I'm not an African, the background is so completely different. You just can't make yourself, so there is no sense putting on and pretending. It's to each his own. I'm not one of these people who have to have a group to hang out with. I guess I have always been a loner. I mean by virtue of the fact that I came from a family of ten, all of whom moved to California except for me. I went to New York and then here.

Do you find that coming from America is an advantage or disadvantage?
I think it's an advantage where you have several things. The American government will look out for you in a pinch, that is the advantage. Another advantage is that generally, at least in Kenya, America is looked on favorably because they have got so much help, and there have been so many people who have been helped personally by American organizations. People have been sent to school by church organizations, so that they have a fairly good opinion of Americans, which is an advantage here, but I think it is maybe a disadvantage in Tanzania.

How many African countries have you visited?
Not many. Tanzania, Uganda, and Kenya.

Which do you like best?
Oh and I've visited Egypt also. I like Kenya better than any.

Was it your decision alone or did your wife have anything to do with coming to Kenya?
Well. She tried to push me but it was up to me. She accepted the fact that I wanted to come to Africa eventually, so that was just a part of her accepting. In fact, we were going to Dar es Salaam. We wanted to. We caught the boat from Egypt and the boat did not stop in Dar es Salaam, it only stopped in Mombasa. So we got off there, and then we had a car with us and drove up to Nairobi and liked it so we decided that we would stay there.

So do you plan to go back to America to live or do you plan on becoming a citizen?
Oh, I don't see why I should go back to America, but I still don't know if I'll become a citizen or not. I'm not fully decided, but I don't see any reason why on the other hand, I have no inclination to go back to America, there is no reason. I mean if things get too hard for me here, but I'm doing more than I could ever possibly do in America. Probably not making as much money as I could in America, but at least I get much more fulfillment. And this is what you work for is achievement. I'm not one of these people who can eventually sit down and hold a job for twenty years or forty years and retire and have nothing to show for it but a paycheck.

How long can you stay in Kenya without becoming a citizen?

Your whole life, there is no requirement that you have to become a citizen.

You must keep getting work permits?

Yes, you have to pay taxes and things like other citizens here. Yes, you have to pay all that. It's no different from aliens living in America. They have to do the same thing—register.

Do you speak any African languages?

No.

What about your daughter?

Yeah, she speaks and understands some Swahili. She and the house girl talk back and forth half English and half Swahili. In fact, she was learning Kikuyu, but we forbade the girl to speak Kikuyu to her because we wanted her to learn Swahili. But the house girl tries to speak English, so it comes out sort of pidgin Swahili-English. But anyway, our little girl, you know children just pick up whatever is said and they can repeat it. They understand as much as they want to understand.

Do you consider yourself a religious, political, or artistic person?

Well, a bit of each. I wouldn't put myself in any one thing. But a bit of each I guess, except political. I may be political in my views but I keep them to myself. Especially in Africa.

Yeah, that's what most people have told me. Why did you have to leave America?

Well, we got tired of it. Really the thing that pushed me was that I got tired of the rat race there. Now I had very good relations with the boss in the office I was working with. We got along fine. He was giving me some jobs to handle on my own, which is kind of special in America for a White firm. But still I realized that I was just sitting there holding a job, pushing a pencil and holding a place there. I wasn't doing anything really.

Did you work in a large firm in the United States?

Yeah. I worked in a large- and middle-size firm. I was doing a lot of housing in New York housing projects. These sort of things, military work.

Does your wife have an interest in architecture?

No more than she gets from me. She has nothing to do with architecture. I'm trying to get her to do some work for me now in one of the buildings I'm doing.

Did you meet her in school in the States?

No, Forty-Second Street. I was just walking down Forty-Second Street in New York, outside Grand Central Station, and I walked up to her and started talking to her and that was it.

So how long have you been married?

Nearly ten years.

So you said that the main reason you left the States was because of the rat race?

Yeah, that was what decided it at the time because I got just tired of dashing to work, sitting in an office in New York where people complained all day long about the job and about the living conditions, day in and day out. You really, really get to see how unhappy it is. I mean the major part of your life is spent in your working office, and if you are not happy, it's absurd.

Some people in discussing the problem in the United States say it's a racial problem. Some say it's an economic one of capitalism. What would you say the major problem in America is?

I think the major problem in America is that America is on the decline. It is coming down, coming apart at the seams. Probably the biggest problem is racial. Americans tried to change, but deep down inside you cut one layer of racialism out and then there is a deeper layer. I think that really among Americans it goes down to the one, that they never get it out. That is one of the things I find wrong with America. Another thing is that America is just a society of liars. Everybody lies, lies, and lies. It's just so embedded that it is sickening. For instance, people say get a telephone call, they would think nothing to telling their kids, tell them I'm not home! But they will go marching with their children to Sunday School on Sunday and think nothing of it. But this is, I really got to see this when I spent a year in Denmark, where people were, at least at that time, far more particular about liars. In fact, they thought less of a liar than anything else. And you really got to see how much that is engrained as a part of America. I think this is the whole problem with American character. Americans are liars. They lie to each other. The big companies lie to the people, the advertisers lie. It's really sickening and it gets worse. It doesn't get better.

I was wondering if you noticed any differences between European and White Americans?

Oh, yes, there is a big difference. According to where you are, because Europeans are very different from one section to another. One little country to another. But I think this is, like I said before, is the thing that characterizes

Americans over all other Europeans. The fact is that the British are big liars too, but they are such more diplomatic about it. I think Americans are much more petty liars. Not only subconsciously they lie to themselves. Then I think this is the big problem with the racial problem. Americans lie to themselves about what they are doing. He's a liberal you know, and deep down inside he's a real, real bigot. That sort of thing.

So you are saying the Europeans are less liars than Americans?
I think that they are more realistic about things than Americans.

Do you think that African consciousness on the part of Afro-Americans is a helpful experience?
Yes, it definitely is. It's a little misleading as you'll find the typical Afro-American when he comes here. I think it has really helped to make a lot of friends with Africans who have gone to the States. And so you find Africans really looking forward to going to the States. And they feel an affinity with American Blacks. This was not there when I was coming up. An African was looked down upon, you did not want to be an African. That was part of the whole propaganda thing in America, but it has changed considerably. Of course, African independence had helped things quite a lot, but it has made a lot of friends for Black Americans in Africa. They really constantly tell you about the good experience they had once.

Which African country do you admire most and why?
Kenya, I admire more than any other because I think that over above everything else, it is a fairly stable country. Even though tribalism here is probably worse than most countries or an awful lot of countries. But still when you look at it and take it as a whole it has done a tremendous amount, and I think, even though it may sound like singing the same old song, a lot of it is attributed to Kenyatta. He is a tremendous person, and I think the feeling goes a long way.

What do you think will happen when he leaves?
That's anybody's guess.

It doesn't frighten you at all?
No, no more than anything else. Everybody has to go some time.

I just wondered if the government would be as stable afterwards?
No, it probably won't. I think the best thing he could do is retire and nominate his successors, and then he would have the prestige of Kenyatta behind him which will enable people more to unite behind the new man. Also President Kenyatta would still have as much say, probably more so.

Do you think a substantial number of Afro-Americans should come to Africa?

No, I don't think a substantial number, comparing to the amount of Afro-Americans there, but I understand there are a lot more in West Africa than in East Africa. East Africa is much newer, and people in the eyes of the United States are just beginning to discover East Africa. I think more and more, I think one day we might get a flood. It's fun as long as people got something to contribute. They don't want people coming here to get on welfare. If you want to get on welfare, stay in the States.

So how do you think they would be accepted by the government and the local people?

I think they will accept them all right. You're always going to have problems. People do have problems and you run into somebody who will give you a hard time and dislike you, but that's anywhere, not just here. I think in general they would be accepted, especially if they have something to contribute.

When you came here to Africa did you have any of the typical misconceptions about life here that Black Americans normally have?

I don't think I really had too many misconceptions. I tried to find out as much about the place as possible. Still there was a problem. The biggest misconception about life here was that I didn't realize how cool it was here in Nairobi. I came over here and I was freezing. I expected it to be better architecturally, but after staying here for a while you understand why it isn't.

Do you think it has improved in the seven years that you've been here?

It's definitely improved a lot of what these old colonialists have left, and that's one thing. You have the fact that the country itself is looking further than just to England. You have to realize that before it had to be English to be right, even if it seemed out of date in England for a thousand years. If it was good enough for England, it was good enough for here as evidence of the school system.

Do you feel like an African, Afro-American, or an American?

When I was here for a short time, I felt more American that I ever did in America. But now it's not nearly so cut and dry.

Do you feel like an African?

How does an African feel? I must say that I'm not treated like an African. It is much harder on the African than on the European, and in that case I think I'm treated much more like a European than like an African.

Would you say you are making an excellent, good, fair, or poor living here?

Fair. It's a lot of work. There is a lot of money here and you can make it. I think probably I'm doing far better than if I had opened my own business in the States. For instance, I've been open now for about one year and three quarters, and I've got about forty-five active jobs going. That is quite substantial, and I don't think I could have moved that quick in the States. Even though I'm not earning much, but you always expect to have a hard time when you open your own office, unless you have a lot of money to carry. Then it's a different story.

Is it very hard to get started when you don't have any money yourself?

It is always anywhere. It's probably easier here than it would be in the States because it doesn't cost as much to operate. Overheads weren't nearly so high, you can operate out of your house here, and so forth, which helps.

What do you envision the future of Africa to be?

The way the population is going I would say crowded in Kenya. Considering it is growing at 3 percent, which is almost as high as anywhere in the world. It will have some pitfalls, but there is nowhere to go but up.

What about the future of Afro-Americans in the States?

In the States, oh, I think will be pretty much the same in a hundred years from now as it is now.

You don't think Black Americans will make progress economically and politically?

Oh, yes, they'll make progress and things will change a bit. But I think a hundred years from now that among those White Americans you'll still have that deep-seated prejudice. You see, it's part of an American's nature to dislike anything that is not like him. You see it in everything, for instance, American science-fiction movies and things like that. What is always the theme? Something comes, and they don't know what it is so they shoot it. This is America's nature and part of that general dislike of others not like yourself as opposed to being conscious to anyone not like myself. The first feeling in America is let's get rid of it 'cause it's not going to change much. Oh, it will change some, maybe things will be much better. I mean it's altogether different. If you see a hotel, you go in and get a meal, and you don't think whether you can go in there or not. Even if you know you can go in there, in the States you still have that feeling. Just the way the headwaiter looks at you, you know what he's thinking. You don't have that here, and if he doesn't want you in there, you can look down your nose at him and say, "Throw me out." Here the government says no segregation. But you don't change people's nature by a decree. Say you're walking down the street in New York, or anywhere else in the States with a White girl. You can feel the people's eyes burning. It's there but not here because you see it all the time, and nobody pays it any attention. Living here you see that it can be, and why isn't it in the States?

You are saying that interracial marriages and romances are more likely to succeed in Kenya than in the United States?

Socially, yes, but you have cultural problems and things like that which cause problems. But socially and publicly—definitely. You see a tremendous amount of mixed couples because you have many Africans who went away to study and really didn't have anybody to marry because there weren't that many African girls educated. So they were at a loss to have a wife who wasn't educated and on their social level. So many brought back wives from where they have studied and it's a very common thing around here.

What do you think the future of your daughter will be now that she was born in Kenya, and she is going to be raised up for the large portion of her life there? How will her life be different from say a young Black girl raised up in the ghetto?

It will be different, and that she has dual citizenship now. She is Kenyan and American, and has to decide for herself, I think, when she is twenty-one. On the other hand, she doesn't come up against the pressure that the girls will have in the States. I think that she probably has no real concept of any kind of racial problem as such. I mean she mixes with African kids, European kids, without any thought of racial problems. She talks about Black and White and hair and all that, but it's just not there, the underlying turmoil is just not here. She will run into it later I guess, and it will probably be much harder for her if she goes to the States 'cause she's not used to it. But I think the way it is now, race means absolutely nothing to her, and there is no reason why it should, living here in Africa. Sure wish I could get some architects out here. I'd like to have one here as a partner right now.

4

Others Who Have Returned

This interview with Mr. Sargenian is enclosed to provide information on an individual who has devoted the bulk of his adult life to working and living in Africa. Although he is not African-American, he is non-White and loves Black life and culture. His illustrations of African people are authentic and precious.

LES SARGENIAN
NOVEMBER 9, 1971

Well, in the first place to identify for your tape, my name is [Les Sargenian], so that you make sure you know who you are talking to, and I come from Massachusetts. I was born in Lawrence, Massachusetts, 1921. And lived there, went to high school, finished my high school there, then I went to Boston and studied art there for three years. And that was just before World War II. And I finished my art school and went straight into the army. And spent three years in Africa, France, Germany, Austria, Italy. I got back to the States in 1945 and 1946, and in '47, '48 was sent to New York City as a commercial advertising illustrator artist.

You worked for a newspaper or magazine there?
I was just a freelance artist, and at that time music was my hobby.

Did you play an instrument?
Yes, I played a number of instruments. Anything I could get my hands on,

you know, to make a living. And, but my many interests in music was always Middle East music.

How did you get interested in that?

Well, I sort of grew up with it in my home. The Middle East music, and I did a lot of research work in music on my own. I carried this on while I was doing my art work. And then in around '48 and '49, I joined a company in Hollywood as a music director, and from there on art has become my hobby and music my profession. So since then I've been with music.

What was the name of the school you were educated at in Boston?

Fesher George School of Art, that's right in the Back Bay area. Right off Huntington Avenue.

And that took three years?

Yes, that was a three-year course.

Where did you first develop an interest in Africa? Was it in the services?

No, for this company in Hollywood. I worked for a while in Hollywood. Then they sent me to Afghanistan and I spent three-and-a-half years there. Collecting folk music, traditional music for background music for films and TV and then I worked in India and Pakistan and in other places in the Far East. Then in the year 1959 the company sent me to Africa, and the first place I went was Ghana. And there, with the aid of Ghanaian musicologists, I traveled over Ghana for about five months, and then I went to Guinea and this was right after their independence. And there I stayed for three-and-a-half years, traveling all over the country making a systematic collection of the music of Guinea, and this was a sort of joint Hollywood and Guinea government project. And while I was there of course I was recording with music. And for that country I recorded a great number of LPs, record albums of music that I had recorded.

Are any of them on the market now?

Yes, it's called in French, of course the title is in French. Translated they mean "New Sounds for a New Nation." And the first album came out in '60 and in '61. We did a few more, in '62 a few more and '63, was when I left Guinea and I went back to the States. And when I returned to the States I was made musical director for the Voice of America for Africa. And went back to Africa, of course, to Liberia where we have our Voice of America radio station, and I was based there for six years. And I used Liberia as my home base, and from there I've traveled throughout practically every country on the continent.

Are you married and have children?

Just my wife. For about ten years she was with me in Africa. We traveled together actually.

And she's back in the States now?

Yes, right.

Have you met any other Black Americans who have decided to spend a great deal of time here in Africa, become expatriates or work here?

Well, in Liberia there are quite a number. In Liberia and there are some in Ghana. I ran across some in Nigeria, I don't recall their name. And let's see. I don't recall if there are any in Senegal. But of course being in Liberia for six years, I knew just about everyone. And that place of course has quite a little closer connection with America, so you find quite a few Americans who have gone there and are living there.

How are they making it? Are they happy there? Do they think much of the United States or do they look upon themselves as Africans?

No, they are happy there, but I think most of them consider themselves Americans. And a lot of them still go back and forth, and of course they can keep dual citizenship which they do. But you know you probably know there was this group of Black Israelites mainly from the Chicago area. I think that the first group was about sixty-five who came out to Liberia to live. And of course when they first came, a small group of them did have a lot of difficulty. They were interviewed and made a lot of noise in the beginning, but then they spread out in the country and from what I understand, the major portion of them were discouraged and most of them have returned back to the States.

What were some of the problems they encountered there that discouraged them?

Well, you see it's a completely different culture. Here Africa and America have nothing to do with color, this is culture. The American Black is an American who is born in American culture. They think differently. They are different people. And going to Africa it's just as much a difference for them as it is for a White man going for the first time to Africa. Well, right here in this country Tom Mboya—the late leader—I think he was the first one to make a public statement that really there's a big difference, the American Black is really not African. Which was interesting. He was probably the first one to make a public statement like that. So this group that came out to Liberia found out that things were a little different from what they expected, and so a number of them did go back.

Now they were Black Jews right?
Yes.

And about how many?
There were sixty-five. Some had stories of the oppression they had in Chicago streets, that U.S. army tanks were down the street shooting people down. And all these many stories.

What was the date they came to Liberia?
This was about three or four years ago. *Time* magazine I think had done an article. I know there was a *Time* magazine man down there doing a story on them.

Were you in Liberia when they came?
Yes, yes.

And you met some?
Yes, some of them were very nice kids.

Were they mostly young?
Yes, they were.

College age?
Yes, mechanics. Some of them were mechanics. Some came. Some of the companies were very good to them. Gave them jobs as secretaries and everybody tried to help as much as possible.

Why didn't they go back to Israel as opposed to Liberia?
Well, I don't know. I don't think Israel was accepting people. I don't think they could go.

Getting back to the whole liberation question. I've heard a lot of talk that when the Black Americans went to Liberia they exploited, or disregarded the native Liberian people creating conflict between the Afro-American who came over and the people who had been there for years.
No, I don't think anymore than the situation that existed between the so-called, which I don't like to use even here because I'm as much opposed to it as President Tubman was, this term Americo-Liberians. As opposed to the local tribal people. But this exists in any country in the world. Any country in Africa you will find these things exist. Something one can almost say that helluva real discrimination among people is not back in the States or anything but right here in Africa itself. Look what happened in Nigeria. And it's gonna take some time yet before some of these tribal feuds. And discrimination between tribes themselves before it's wiped out. It's unfortunate but that's the situation, and these Americans who have come here have ex-

ploited the local people. They have come. They have opened up legitimate businesses and they have tried to make a living, and in fact I think one can say they have contributed. They have contributed to the country.

By being in Africa what do you miss most about America?

Well, I'm really not a type that question is good for because as an American official working for the U.S. government overseas in most countries we have good housing and we usually have everything available and in most countries you can get most everything whether it is food wise or clothing wise. And where both my wife and I have never really missed anything. Really no difference from the way we were living in the States. And everybody misses, of course, their own home, your family and relatives and things like that. But actually any great difficulty of missing things of your everyday living, I would say no. We haven't missed anything.

Have your conceptions of America changed at all as a result of being in Africa for these years? Do you look at America in a different light, or is it the same?

Well, I think we have the same feelings as anybody who travels abroad.

You mentioned that President Julius Nyerere in Tanzania invited you there twice?

No, it wasn't the president. It was the Tanzanian radio invited me there a couple of years ago. We traveled throughout the country taking samples of Tanzanian music. And I helped the music department of the radio there. Working along with them.

Have you ever thought of becoming a citizen in some of the African countries?

No, I wouldn't think of it. I was born in America. That's my home, my country. I wouldn't think of going and living. I would have no reason to. Because I think that a man who would move or go away and give up his citizenship and become a citizen of another country, I think that he should be doing that with the intention that he's going to contribute to that country. And right now the way my work is I'm contributing to all of Africa and not just to one country. And I'm also contributing to my own country. My knowledge that I do bring back of Africa to my country. As you realize too and everybody should realize, we are now in a stage on this earth, damned, we've come to the place where everybody got to know more about each other. This is really my whole pleasure in my work and my real purpose. That's why I'm satisfied with what I'm doing. And I don't think I would benefit myself or any country by going and becoming a citizen of another country.

Do you think that Africa consciousness on the part of Afro-Americans is a helpful experience?

Think so very much. I'm all for it. I'm for these Black students that are being encouraged in the United States, and especially the Black people in the United States. I think this a great benefit for the Afro-American to know about Africa.

Do you think that a substantial number of Black Americans should come to Africa to settle?

If they have a reason to, yes, but not just for the idea of trying to identify themselves as Africans and the idea of just coming to live in Africa unless they really have. I don't know if they really have any need to do this. Unless they come temporarily to learn about Africans and contribute something to Africa and contribute something of their own people back in the United States. Then that's OK, but just the idea of leaving the United States to come live in Africa. I don't see any reason for it.

How do you think Afro-Americans would be accepted if they came to live here?

Well, it still goes back to what I've been trying to say about contribution. I think they would be accepted very well by African countries if these people are coming to contribute their knowledge, and knowledge that would help these universities. Especially teachers in schools. Black American teachers come out to Africa, I think they would be welcomed in any country. I don't think any wouldn't want them. But just for the idea that some say they have been disillusioned with the country where they were born and want to come and now live in Africa. African people are very sensitive people, and there is a great possibility that they wouldn't accept some of the Black Americans. Because maybe the Black Americans wouldn't fit into the way of living.

What do you envision the future of the Afro-American to be in the States?

Well, I think we're on the right course in America. I believe in it very much. I think we're the only country where I think we are on the right course, both the Black and the White Americans. All these things that have been happening all these years and still, I think they helped, demonstrations, things have helped, and I think we are doing something about it. And it will take some time but you can't wipe, well, this is all over the world. There will be differences in every country that's doing something about. I think we're on the right road.

ABA-LA McHARDY[1]
JANUARY 20, 1999

When the late Kwame Nkrumah led Ghana to political independence in 1957, African-Americans and others in the diaspora believed that a new era of autonomy was dawning on the African continent. Many activists and scholars, such as the Harvard-trained W.E.B. Du Bois repatriated to Ghana where he worked as a close associate and advisor until his death in 1963. McHardy, who lived and worked in Ghana during the first decade of Ghana's independence, shares through her interview a firsthand account of this historical period in Pan-African history.

Where were you born? Should I refer to you as Aba or Miss McHardy?
Call me Aba-La. I am a Buddhist lama. My given name is Cecile McHardy.

So, where were you born, Aba-La?
I was born in Jamaica. I went to England to study at the University of London, School of Estate Management. I lived and worked in England for a couple years and then I went to work in Nigeria in 1953. I worked for African Principals Entrepreneurs in timber logging and rubber plantations. I was based in Sapele, Nigeria in Ondo province, the heart of a tropical rain forest. It was an interesting and inspiring experience. Africans were in competition with the big multinationals, such as Unilever Company, Companie Française Afrique Occidental, which monopolized the shipping and import and export trades. They had large concessions to exploit the forest reserves.

Was this your first time going to Africa?
Uh-hmm.

At that time did you view yourself as an African or a Jamaican?
I'm a Maroon, my origins are people who resisted slavery by running away and we achieved our freedom in 1738 in Jamaica. As you know, some of our people capitulated upon terms and were tricked and shipped to Halifax in Canada where they refused to work. They claimed status of prisoners of war. Finally, they were sent back to Africa to Sierra Leone. So, in my own personal family history, I am an Afro-American in the diaspora, a Pan-African.

So, when you went to Nigeria, did you see yourself as a Maroon or did you see yourself as an African?
No, I saw myself as a human being! I claim my Native American, Arawak, Taino, Carib heritage just as I claim the European, Spanish, Scottish,

[1]Name has not been altered.

Sephardic Jew heritage, just as I claim African heritage. It is racism in the world that distinguishes and wants to limit our humanity, and cultural legacies. But I see myself as a new human being. An example of the evolution of a new human being in the world, representing a complex consciousness.

Did you have this view of yourself at this early stage of your life?

Strong identification with that. Of course, because Pan-Africans contributed in the defense of two world wars, while we remained still dependent colonial territories, my experience in Nigeria clarified for me how exploitative, how oppressive was colonial rule.

You were working with management in this timber company when you went to Nigeria?

It was a timber and rubber estate, a vast enterprise. It was a family-owned enterprise and I was involved in commodity marketing through brokers in the principal European capitals and in the United States.

Did you see yourself as being part of the exploiting class—the colonials?

No, no! I met few European expatriates. We did not use the racist language of Black and White then. I too was an expatriate. I was privileged. Paradoxically I was politicized by my experience in Nigeria. I was enraged by the political and economic exploitation which colonial rule involved. The neglect. The waste. I was trained in economics and it was obvious there was no attempt to help us form institutions, for example, to encourage domestic capital markets. It's ironic that today people speak of the corruption in Nigeria, the scandal of billions of dollars and other foreign currencies simply stashed under people's beds. As entrepreneurs operating out of Sapele, I remember we got little banking "services." The British colonial banks like Barclays existed solely to negotiate documents and provide us with specie. If you had 3,000 rubber laborers as we did, you could not pay them in paper. They wanted coins, as money would disintegrate in the rain. Modern Nigeria's been carefully socialized by internalizing the colonial values of British financial institutions.

Why did you leave?

My contract had expired. I thought I was going to pursue my academic studies. Then I thought maybe I'd write about my African experience first. I went and I lived for two years in Italy. Did a grand tour of France, Spain, Germany, Denmark, Austria, Yugoslavia. I know Italy inch by inch and Sicily. I studied Italian in Perugia. I fell in love with Italy, its language, its landscape, its art. It was a spiritual home to me. Italians had an aesthetic appreciation for color. I encountered no racism there.

How was that?

Oh, it was fine. Fine. Privileged Black, you know. That's the days when Josephine Baker is in France and Bricktops, the celebrated jazz entertainer, had a salon I frequented in Italy. No, I was a privileged, educated, economically independent young woman. Ghana had become independent, and it was at the Commonwealth Prime Ministers conference in 1957, while I was on a visit to London that Ghanaians invited me to some function, a screening of the film *Freedom for Ghana*. It was a documentary on Ghana's independence. I met some of Nkrumah's top advisers, one of whom was Sir Robert Jackson, who was at that time one of his last trusted expatriate advisors.

He was from where?

From Australia, had been a Commander in the navy, knighted by the British, and married to Barbara Ward, the economist, who became the Baroness of Lodesworth. She was my dear and valued friend and mentor. She lived half the year in Ghana, and did extended lecture tours around the world, was one of the distinguished editors of the British journal, the *Economist*. So, when I met the Jacksons they said you should come to Ghana. So, I got an offer to work in the presidential office in Ghana.

You're working in Nkrumah's office, president of newly independent Ghana. What was that like to work closely with him?

I lived in Ghana and worked for the Government for ten years in a variety of capacities, was frequently included on delegations: to the USSR (women's movement), the Afro-Asian Conference in Tashkent (writers), the inaugural session of the OAU in Ethiopia (Pan-Africa), the Tri-Continental Conference in Cuba (African diaspora). I was one of the organizing secretaries, with Drs. Kenneth Dike, Nana Nketsia Lalage Bown, Michael Crowther, William Abrahams, Thomas Hodgkin, for the First International Conference of Africanists held in Ghana in 1962. I worked in the Institute of Art and Culture, associated with establishing a vital School of Music and Drama and African Studies at the University of Legon, Ghana Film and Radio; museums, Writers' Society; the Padmore Library, etc. The Presidential Office was in Christiansborg Castle. It's a magnificent architecture, built by the Danes in 1690, with lovely inner courtyards, whitewashed walls, gardens, dramatic panoramic views of the sea. I get impatient with Afro-Americans who visit these old castles and only see the slave barracoons. They were elegant residences of factors and governors, as spacious as European castles I have visited in Scotland which, incidentally, have been preserved with their elegant interior furnishings, dungeons and all.

The cabinet meetings were held in the Castle. I engaged in typing, repro-
duced and distributed Cabinet Papers—so had interaction with the Cabinet
ministers, and their staff, the parliamentary secretaries, the permanent
secretaries, regional reps and traditional chiefs, etc. Also official guests
were often hosted/accommodated at Christiansborg Castle which also
served as the Prime Minister's Residence. There were three other
women—we were secretaries, today you'd say personal assistants—did a
lot of the donkey work and got to know everybody. I remember when we
hosted Indira Gandhi.

What role did Nkrumah see the diaspora playing in Ghana?
   OK, so Richard Wright visits C.L.R. James and George Padmore, some
of his close advisors. He invites Du Bois to come. George Padmore comes
to run his African Affairs Bureau. Ras Makonnen's really involved in aiding
the liberation of the rest of Africa. So, we hosted a lot of conferences. You
may remember the 1958 Pan-African Congress attended by Tom MBoya
and Lumumba of the Congo, before Congo's independence, representatives
of youth movements, trade unions, women's organizations, burgeoning political parties, coming together to prepare an agenda for the future of an independent Africa. So there was that level of organizing in terms of a big
vision for Africa, not just for Ghana. We understood that Ghana's independence was meaningless unless linked to the total liberation of Africa. Ghana
was a little country, relative to the vastness and complexity of Africa. There
was a lot of effort to form larger political groupings. We did form a union
with Guinea. It was important to unite with contiguous states. So, Bourkina
Faso and Côte d'Ivoire and Togo were candidates for such regional coop-
eration because the hydro-electric power which would be produced by the
famous hydro-electric station, the Volta River Dam, would have produced
more electricity than we could use. If we had a union, then the contiguous
states could use it to industrialize. So, there were those efforts. Then, with
Du Bois' initiative, we hosted in 1962 the First International Congress of
Africanists. We were associated with Dr. Kenneth Dike who was Vice
Chancellor of the University of Ibadan and Michael Crowther. Among others present were Melville Herskovits who wrote *Myth of the African Past*. It
was a big event. It was an initiative associated with writing definitive
works—a work which we intended would take many years, for an *Encyclo-
pedia Africana*, which Skip Gates has now inherited here at Harvard. The
fourth initiative would have been the establishment of the Organization of
African Unity, OAU. Its plenary conference was held in Addis Ababa in
1962. I was on the delegation to the first meeting of the OAU.

And Nkrumah played a key role in the OAU.

It was a collaborative effort of the independent states of Africa at that time. Nkrumah had a vision and other people shared and supported it. It was a big vision of the organization building Pan-African institutions. Lots of good relationships developed with Nasser in Egypt because they had achieved independence before we did, and had experience in confrontation with the colonial powers when he nationalized the Suez Canal with all the problems that brought about.

So, here you are, in your mid 20s in Ghana. By that time had you developed a sense of your place in the diaspora? Did Nkrumah help in this development?

I take exception to how your question seems to foster a cult of personality, a misunderstanding of political leadership, personalize policy as "Nkrumah did this and that." He had a host of managers and advisors, his vision was a shared vision. In some measure he was their creature and we must acknowledge the inspiration that Garvey's movement provided, and it was not only Pan-Africans. Barbara Ward, the economist, was a close friend and advisor and was instrumental in securing President Kennedy's support for the Volta River Project and the Valco Aluminum Smelter—a multi-million-dollar project which could not proceed unless the United States government guaranteed the foreign investment principals against nationalization of their assets. But yes, Nkrumah appreciated the value of communicating with Africans in the diaspora and in soliciting their support in fulfilling the political agenda—total liberation of Africa. Nkrumah appreciated the role Maroon resistance played as a precursor of revolution in the New World. He was familiar with C.L.R. James's seminal work, *The Black Jacobins*, and the role the Maroons played in the independence of Haiti. I was very proud and inspired to have been involved with Ghana in the early years of its independence. It had very enlightened policies. We had an excellent Children's Library and a mobile one, with sensitive selections of books appropriate for post-colonial African children. The education system was excellent, secondary schools were based upon the British model. Achimota was intended to educate an African elite for leadership, and the Universities of Legon and Kumasi began to provide higher education, with an emphasis on medicine and the sciences. There were the right priorities. We established an Africana library later known as the Padmore Library and sent young Ghanaians off to study library science. Cultural life was sophisticated—we had a Writers' Society and hosted Chinua Achebe and Wole Soyinka, J. P. Clark, South African writers like Zik Mphelele, Louis Nkosi. It was not a backwater. The Public Radio Program—we reviewed books, plays, films. There was a Drama Studio in Accra. I remember Maya Angelou producing Brecht plays. She acted in *Mother Courage.*

While in Ghana, did you see yourself as a Garveyite?

I don't like to identify as Garveyite, you know, because that again sounds cultist. Because Garvey simply represented a consciousness that was shared. If you go and you read Portuguese, you read Brazilian writers or you read writers from Colombia and so on, you will find that there is a shared human historical experience that legitimatizes, for one example, how early Africans were here. We were here long before the Pilgrim fathers, the Boston Brahmans. We were here in the New World long before North America is settled. You must remember, Spanish colonization had a monopoly in the Americas for 150 years, from 1492, 'til what is it? 1619, when the Mayflower comes, 127 years. You have Blacks who have now peopled the Caribbean, Central America, Mexico, and South America because that was the world that the Spanish dominated, long before the North Europeans came. It includes Florida and parts of Texas and so on, California. Blacks are here long before North European immigrants. Then it would be Native Americans, the Hispanics, and us—Omni-Americans.

Let me back up, because I referred to you as a Garveyite. I don't want to make it sound like a cult, but you had this consciousness at a very early age, while African-Americans tended to be very slow in adopting this consciousness.

All right, the difference between the people from the Caribbean and Mexico, that is Afro-Americans from the Caribbean, Central America, Mexico, and South America, with the exception of Brazil and Cuba, is that we achieved emancipation from slavery earlier than the U.S.A. We had access to land. It's the Maroon consciousness that I'm speaking about, and I don't like to make Maroons either as a little cult. It's a kind of consciousness. So, people always knew that there were some of us who had crossed over, been liberated, were in Africa as missionaries, teachers, traders. Angela Davis wrote a piece when she was in prison about the role of women during slavery. "They were custodians of a house of resistance." Slave or free, you hear it in Black Christianity, you hear it in Black Islam, meaning like the Nation of Islam, an uncompromising contestation about the truth of our survival, of our glorious survival. Not as victims, though the struggle is not yet over, but there were people who knew the truth going all the way back to our connections with Egypt and the Queen of Sheba. I come from a generation who knew that. It wasn't a question of identity with Africa. We were there in Africa as revolutionaries to aid in its liberation from colonial rule. We were there as humanists. Obviously, some of us were so easily distinguished by the color of our skins, but to limit as Derek Walcott would say, lots of others would say, to limit, you see there's no way that I can identify with any single African culture because all of it inheres in me or none. I can't say I'm more Ghanaian than I am Dahomian or Yoruba, Akan, Wolof, Bambara, Mandingo, whatever, or Senegalese. My study of Maroons was to trace cultural continuities in the New World. I didn't want to trace it to establish some glorified cultural artifact or something like that, but it was about this creative consciousness. An enlightened consciousness of what it means to be human. So, I end up being a Buddhist lama. That was what I was chasing, and that was what I connected with when I was in Africa. When I went to Nigeria, I remember my principal whose education had probably ended when he was thirteen or fourteen in public school, elementary school that was provided at that time. He ends up being an entrepreneur. His concern about ecology, now this is the '50s in a colonial regime, when he says, "God will punish us if we don't put back something where we take out these beautiful, wonderful trees." More than that, he was a posthumous child of a traditional Yoruba priest. Meaning he was in his mother's belly when his father died. So, I swear to you, Joseph Asaboro was his name, told me he used to dream, because we used to do logging in the Niger Delta. We used to log Abura, it's a tree like a cedarwood, aromatic wood, a very lovely timber. It grows in swamp, so it was hard for the tree enumerators to go in to identify which species to log and then to cut it, and you have to float the logs out. You need lots of gangs of lumberjacks to bring it out. I remember going in with a tree unit, because I was interested in stuff like this, and you would see oily water, you know, and Joseph used to say, he used to dream of oil derricks on the shore, that oil was there. This is long before the possibility of drilling for oil in that part of the world. But in terms of a recognition of the resources that people often talk about Africa and how poor it is, and to ignore the immense resources it represents, and I mean like physical resources, I'm not even just talking about the human resources. Oil in southern Sudan, diamonds in Sierra Leone, the immense mineral wealth in the Congo—all the areas of conflict.

When did you first develop an interest in Africa?

As a child. My mother was a close associate of both Garvey's wives, Amy Jacques, and Amy Ashwood, ardent feminists and social activists and I was socialized by a host of these distinguished, educated, independent women—Ethlyn Rhodd, Florence Case, Amy Bailey, et al. Amy Jacques Garvey was very influential in my childhood. She was a private secretary to Ethiopia's Emperor Haile Selassie in London and influential in mobilizing

Pan-Africans for defense of Ethiopia's war against fascist Italians. I received my early education about Africa in the Caribbean and in my teens worked at the University College of the West Indies in the Registrar's office, at the exciting time of its genesis in 1949.

When you went to Nigeria, did you meet any other African-Americans working there in Nigeria?
No, not in the '50s. In the '60s scholars like Martin and Marion Kilson, friends of Azikiwe.

Were you in Ghana at the time that Du Bois died?
Uh-hmm.

What was that like?
I was with my daughter and Nana Nketsia IV who was Vice Chancellor at Legon University. We went to see Du Bois three days before he died. I remember being touched because representatives from the Chinese embassy were also there visiting. They had thoughtfully brought him a little covered dish with corn, young steamed corn, which they remembered he liked.

So, you saw Du Bois about three days before he died?
Uh-hmm.

Was he ill three days before?
Uh-hmm. We knew he was ailing.

What was the illness that he had?
I don't remember. He was old then and very feisty. Off the record, I remember his joking with his wife, Shirley, implying he still was active sexually. A young man mentally and a delightful person.

So, when he finally passed, what did that mean to you personally?
Old people die. Death is natural. No, much more. What it meant to Nkrumah and to Pan-Africanism was the issue. You see Nkrumah was a young man. His policies were not full-blown from his own head. He had advisors and guidance from elders and so on. When Du Bois died, when George Padmore died, it was a great loss to Africa because Nkrumah lost confidants and guides, trusted advisors who were very important in his political maturation.

Did you attend the funeral of Du Bois?
I think all of Accra did.

You showed me a photograph of his casket with Shirley Du Bois and Nkrumah looking on.
Ghana was the kind of place when Muhammad Ali is passing through to

go and fight in Zaire, I mean, the plane is just stopping in Accra, all of the city turns out to see him. In that sense, community relationships, social cohesion, the importance of full participation of the extended family, the social protocols associated, as you know, with death, are very, very elaborately done. Some poor person dies and their great ambition was to have a Mercedes, and some woodcarver carves a wooden Mercedes as the coffin. It's that kind of world. Fulfill your life's desires, even in death.

So, after Du Bois' death, Kwame Nkrumah wrote in Dark Days in Ghana, *that the U.S. government had something to do with his being deposed. Was that a fair assessment?*

I was away from Ghana on a UNESCO travel fellowship in 1964/1965 which enabled me to engage in preliminary research for a study of the history of the Maroons, principally archival research in the Caribbean (Cuba, Haiti, Jamaica, Puerto Rico, Trinidad), Suriname, Guiana, Brazil, Mexico, and the USA. I had extensive interviews with scholars in the field, and surveyed the resources at the Schomburg Collection, Columbia University Libraries, the Research Institute for the Study of Man, collections at Roosevelt College (Chicago), Northwestern University (Evanston), University of Wisconsin (Madison), Indiana University (Bloomington), the Library of Congress, the Moorland Foundation Collection at Howard University, the Peabody Museum Library at Harvard, and the Library of the Caribbean Organization in Puerto Rico. I was away for a year. The Cold War was very intense in Africa, and, in particular, Ghana. We were on a socialist path. When Ghana committed troops in the Congo as an initiative, we hoped that the U.N. would back it up or other nations would provide military support to Lumumba. The troops that were sent were people trained in the British colonial army, they were not political. As you know, it's very hard to have a coup by people trained by the British because of the loyalty thing, and the soldiers are not partisans. They serve the nation, and the legitimate head of state. It was those people who were sent to the Congo, and they had a hard time. It was a vast tropical rain forest, no infrastructure. Ghana's army was about 8,000 at the time. I was very much involved through the Ministry of Culture in an endeavor which was called The Worker's Brigade. We had a quarter of a million young people who needed to be incorporated into the labor force. Some of them would have had two or three years of formal schooling if any. Half of them were intended to be an agricultural labor force; the other half to be industrial work force. They needed skills training and they also needed discipline and so on. The United States provided technical assistance in establishing the Brigade, based on the model of the Civil Conservation Corps associated with TVA, Tennessee Valley Project, and the WPA New Deal model.

Yes.

Anyway, The Worker's Brigade, they were not armed, but they were seen as a possible paramilitary force which could displace the regulars if armed. I mean, we had officers who helped train them. Some became tailors and shoemakers because they had to have uniforms and shoes. Some of them learned to cater, cook, and grow food. We were very involved in their cultural activities and entertainment. So, that's the genesis of our national dance troupe and our national orchestra and so on, created from people from The Worker's Brigade. Young people from all over, and it was very important in terms of nation building because people used to say, Ewe drummers can't drum like Ashanti drummers, and we set out to prove in fact that music is music and it can be learned. This is where I said the university was pivotal. Its school of music and drama, its school of African studies pioneered this interface with the people. We sent people to be trained in circus arts in China, the USSR. UNESCO sent us dramaturgs to assist in producing and presenting theatre arts. Nkrumah's praetorian guards; his border guards and presidential guards came now from these new young people. It was said that his border guards and presidential guards were given more modern weapons and so on and that they had sent the old guards and the people who were trained by the colonials to be cannon fodder in the Congo. The quarter million force of the Workers Brigade represented a possible threat to the traditional army if they were ever around for civil defense. And so it was a class struggle, and so when they came back from the Congo, there were those social groups which had legitimate quarrels and they were aided by America. America was very involved.

CIA?

Don't say. Won't say. And it was a bloodless coup. Consequently they allowed the Prime Minister's wife and children to leave. Nkrumah was away on a visit to see Ho Chi Minh in Vietnam. He took refuge in Guinea. Yes, I have no doubt of that. Anybody who had any sense knows that it was a consequence principally of our involvement in the Congo which put our soldiers in harm's way in the defense of that strange and violent place. Also a lot of Ghana's wealth at the time, because Ghana had a lot of reserves when it became independent and the cocoa price was good and so on. And a lot of Ghana's wealth was used, in supporting liberation movements in Africa. So some Ghanaians had resentments about that. I mean, we ferried out a lot of

South Africans, intellectuals and activists, and our attorney general, Geoffrey Bing and his wife were involved a lot in getting out ANC people. That's when Maya Angelou, if you remember, who was married to a South African ANC member in Cairo, came to Ghana.

So after Nkrumah was deposed, how long did you stay in Ghana? Did you leave right afterwards?

Actually, I was away for a year before the coup. When I got back to Ghana, shortly after, it would be about three months after I got back, there was the Tri-Continental Conference called by President Fidel Castro in Cuba. I had been in Cuba earlier because Cuba has done a lot of work on Maroon studies. They call them "Apalençados" from Palenque, which is a Mayan name for sanctuary. I went to that conference. Two weeks after my return the coup occurred. I left government service and worked for the Volta Aluminum Company for a year before I was deported. It was a consortium of Kaiser Aluminum, Reynolds, Alcan. I was personal secretary to the production manager. The factory was just about to go on line. It was going to be our first smelt. Anyway, I remember this intelligence officer coming through, and he recognized me. I remember our eyes met. I don't think it was Valco because they were very helpful, but Ghana security people that evening hand-delivered a letter that we had twenty-four hours to leave the country, myself and my eight-year-old daughter.

Did they give you reasons why they wanted you to leave?

None. They were declaring other expatriates persona non grata. But I suspected, you see, because I had films, I had tapes of recordings I had made when I had done my research on the African Diaspora. I think they must have gone through my stuff and thought I was giving intelligence to Nkrumah who was then making radio broadcasts from Guinea. And then also I think the correspondence about getting his book, *Neocolonialism: The Last Stage of Imperialism*, published in Spanish, like when they go through the presidential papers and they find my letters in my own handwriting, stuff like that. It was a shock because it wasn't fair, because I would have served any government. I would have continued serving Ghana. I became a refugee. I left all my goods and chattel and I was not permitted to go back. I continued to visit Africa frequently, but not until twenty-five years later did I go back to Ghana.

So where did you go?

I went to France.

And what year was that, that you left?

Let's see, '66, '67, in '67. Then I worked for Présence Africaine, the first African publishing house established by Alioune Diop which first brought to the world's notice the works of Franz Fanon.

And what did you do at Présence Africaine?

I was a contributing editor. So I was in France with my daughter for, I don't know, eighteen months or so and then my old mentor, Barbara Ward, had the Schweitzer Chair at Columbia University. She heard about my refugee status and was instrumental in my getting a fellowship to Harvard. So I came to Harvard from Paris in 1968. . . .

'68. And that was your first time?

And I've been here ever since.

So that was when you first came to the States.

No, I was here in '64 on a UNESCO Fellowship when I was doing my research on Maroon societies and I met St. Clair Drake, all the old scholars, Herskovitz's old students, all the people who had done work with him when he was at University of Chicago. In fact, when I went to Mexico, I met Aguirre Bertran, another of Professor Herskovitz's distinguished Mexican students. I even have books inscribed by him to me. I became a U.S. citizen. I taught at Goddard for ten years.

Did your perception of America change as a result of being in Africa?

I was an ignorant anti-American. In Paris, I knew people like Chester Himes and Richard Wright who fled this place because their relatives were lynched. We from the Caribbean used to think the USA was an ugly, awful place because of these iniquities. We knew it was a dangerous place to be if you were Black, even if you were privileged. I came here when Martin Luther King was killed during the civil rights movement, the anti-Vietnam War movement. I was invited to come and teach at Goddard College to establish a Black studies program, and I fought it, because I said there's nothing called Black studies. You can have African studies; you can study the African Diaspora. I remember being very adamant, and I didn't think that it was a field of study for Blacks only. I thought it was a legitimate part of American history. I still do. And I fought it. I said, I want to teach this stuff to everybody. The program was funded for only two years. The Black studies program closed, and I was invited to stay on to be a full faculty member. I had a positive message from the very beginning, saying, forget about the slavery part and talk about the part where we triumphed, where we resisted. And we resisted successfully because we're still here. I represent people who resisted, who are still here, and if you want to find authentic African cultural continuities, you're going to find it among people who resisted, and they're also going to be finding it in secret societies or rather societies with secrets, because we haven't yet fully triumphed. Because as humanists our struggle is not only about us, and the people who are interrogating whiteness today are beginning to hold that view. And it needs to be challenged because they want to abolish affirmative action saying it represents reverse discrimination. One of the ways that you fight that argument is to have Whites interrogate whiteness and demand reparations. Reparations before repatriation would be my priority. Anybody who identifies as White has false consciousness, because there's no such thing as White people, just as there's no such thing as Black people. It's possible to celebrate diversity, infinite diversity, the richness of diversity and difference.

Today, do you consider yourself a religious person, a political person, artistic person, or all of the above?

Identity! Labels are so limiting! I don't see how you can separate them. I think we are an extraordinary people. I think values, the human values that inhere in us, you know, without judgment of oppressor and oppressed and all of the lived experience, what makes for the compassion, what makes for the forgiveness, what makes for the love, truthful appreciation of our interconnected past. What makes us speak truth to power is consciousness, awareness that spiritual insight makes no distinction between "them and us." When we are talking about Africans who sold Africans to the New World or whatever, it's an interdependent world and there's a flux and reflux.

What do you mean by flux and reflux?

Well, your theme is about repatriation, who went back. We brought it with us. And wherever you go, there you are. And if you are a moral, compassionate human being, you will manifest those qualities wherever you are. And so, Africans left Africa and came to the New World, and some flew back and forth, go back and forth. Our children go back and forth, and we also have intermingled with all the other people in the world. It's like a family extending.

This sounds like a "we are the world" theme. You seem to suggest that African people should forgive the European for slavery, segregation, and discrimination?

Yes. It's dualistic to separate "them and us." They are all my ancestors. Yes, understand our past. To understand is to forgive. There is a triumph of the spirit to be able to forgive, and I think that this is what Pan-African consciousness represents. Our joyousness, our capacity to be creative. We even take bad things to make laughter. We sing the blues, we scream, and we are violent in our orature, and then we calm down and make carnival—a celebration, a capacity for creative joy. We have shared this with the world. Anna Deavere Smith was here last summer and there was a feast. And there was this young woman who just sang the American national anthem, or "America the Beautiful." Her voice claimed it. This beautiful rich divided land that struggles in its triumphs. I think America, meaning the New World, represented something new for the twentieth century. I don't know if we'll be tops for the twenty-first century, but yeah. Remarkable things happened here in terms of scale of community and consciousness.

But when you reflect back on the days when you were in Africa, do you consider those days as highlights to your life?

I am proud. I am proud of those young people who came from the New World to assist in that endeavor. The vision was great. I am proud and I see even a manifestation of idealism when you can have South Africa emerge as it did without a bloodbath. A maturity, I don't know, a lightness. A lesson to the world. So, yes. And I've been disappointed with a lot that has happened since, but time is long as the proverb goes "no matter how grown up you are, how tall you grow, your eyes never grow higher than your eyebrows." And it has to do with, I think, spiritual maturity. Life is good anyway, you know. Even the suffering is useful. I am proud of the ancestry, the lineage.

Do you think a substantial number of Black Americans should repatriate to Africa? Or settle in Africa?

Well this is not a new notion. It has always been happening. People who were integrated into African life in Ethiopia, (Rastas) were religious, learned Amharic, had artistic skills, weaving, leatherwork, gardening, rearing stock. Similarly in Ghana there are traditions of people from Jamaica settling in Mampong credited with the creation of the Botanical Gardens at Aburi. My generation, I suspect, went to serve, to contribute something. There was less the notion that we went to settle. The West African coastal states were not "settler" colonies, arguably. The climate is challenging to health. People "settled" in the salubrious Kenya Highlands, South Africa. People lived in Morocco and Tunisia. Many of us had children who were born in Africa of African parentage. So we had established normal links. Perhaps if I gave a short list of the Pan-African expatriates who I knew in Ghana, who came to serve: Julian Mayfield, a novelist, came to work on one of the national newspapers, with his wife Lydia Cordera, a pediatrician who worked in Public Health—were there with their children; Julia Wright, Richard Wright's daughter and her French husband, Henry Hervé, also journalists with their children; people who worked for the UN and other international agencies who served and went to serve in other countries; Vilma Scott and her children, husband a mathematician concerned with census statistics; UN functionary, Leslie Lacy and Sylvia Boone Smith, graduate students in African Studies Program at the University of Legon, both published; theatre people like Morisseau LeRoy from Haiti and Roberto Blanco from Cuba who went to serve in Senegal and Angola. Academics: Jan Carew from University of Chicago; Edward Brathwaite worked in the Ministry of Education, Ed Brathwaite wrote "To Sir With Love." Bob Lee and his wife were dentists in private practice. Many of us who were there in the '50s and '60s would love to still be there.

What kept you from returning?

Political instability. The volatile nature of neocolonialism made it difficult. And many of us shared the fate even of Ghana nationals who went into exile. For us, the decision was choiceless since we were expelled. It was twenty-five years before I could return to Ghana, though I frequented other parts of Africa.

Is there still a problem in returning?

The situation changed in the '80s and '90s. People like Isaac Hayes are embraced, initiated and empowered, inducted into traditional lineages, made Chiefs which confers access to land. Or Jake Williams of "An Oil Dynasty" fame for his services was honored by traditional titles which is one way of being formally reintegrated into traditional society.

What contributions can African-Americans make to Africa today?

I think that there are very variable contributions which African Americans can make. In fact, they have been and can be a very powerful influence. Millions of people watch the *Cosby Show*. So, I think there are opportunities in publishing and education and media, education particularly like what Renee Neblett is doing with Distance Learning. Lots of economic opportunities. My daughter Alero builds schools, housing, condos, just like what we have in Miami. Live in Boston and Arizona and whatever, but have residences in Africa. And Africa represents a new important market for a lot of things. Can have an edge over other expatriates.

So, why do you reject repatriation?

I do not. It has always been happening. I do think we should claim a wider world. I think—my daughter lives in Scotland. When we were refugees and Africa was in terrible turmoil, it ended up that she couldn't go to school in Ghana anymore, and I didn't want her to move here, because they were killing Blacks. I didn't like the racism here. We have Scottish ancestors. My name is McHardy. I have a Scottish grandfather. My cousins married Scots and so on. I mean we consider ourselves Blacks, colored folk or whatever. And we have a lot of colored folk, and there have always been a lot of colored folk. Go and look at Dabydeen's work on Hogarth's *London in the Eighteenth Century*. Go and look at Elizabethan days and see. We've always been here, there, and everywhere. I mean why should I let Alexander Hamilton claim a piece of America and not me? He was born in Nevis you know. And I claim a piece of the United States of America and will not give it up. This is an interdependent world. Wait until we get on with my Asian claims, because my sister married a Chinese, and my brother-in-law married an Indian. You want me to compartmentalize these networks? Its my social capital. Why should we? It's an advantage.

Do you think African-Americans would be accepted by the Africans and the African governments if they repatriated?

Look at the historical record. One can't generalize. Africa is too vast and complex. A lot depends on the attitude. One should go with no arrogance and great curiosity and willingness to learn an African language. And there is a tendency we have, you see, that if you can't read and write you are an idiot. We equate literacy with intelligence. At the same time we do not appreciate being bilingual. In my encounter with Africa in the village, I often encountered people who couldn't read or write, but they were eloquent, fluent in more languages. Multilingual, not simply bilingual. It has to do with a great reciprocity of respect, and that everybody has a story. Everybody has different knowledge. I remember in Ghana when we were trying to get the shamen to share their knowledge, and they would say, you know, this is the knowledge that all the members of my lineage have. This is knowledge of my lineage, my family. And we'd say, "Well, what is it?" And he says, "One I've inherited. And it's a knowledge of how to heal bones." Because at first we think it's mumbo jumbo. If you come from the West you think it's "voodoo." Very practical. It's to heal fractured bones. If you have multiple fractures, they know how to heal it. And they break it up, and they use the marrow from the Aguti, from the mongoose, and they make a styptic, and they use a special clay and marijuana to make a cast. And they keep on breaking and massaging the limb. So, they're using bone marrow. And this one village has this protocol as their secret. And they're healers, and they're renowned. I mean, football players who break their thighs, and Western doctors say they can't play again, because they limp. And they go into this village and they do it. It takes a long time. That's inherited knowledge.

Did they share this knowledge with you?

Yes, to an extent. The shaman tells me about when he was a small boy. He sees two venomous snakes fighting. Different species. One bites the other. Its mate comes and eats that leaf and that leaf and that leaf and goes and gives it to its mate. "So," he says, "I used the venom from the snake and that leaf and that leaf and that leaf as an antidote to the toxin of a venomous snake, and it works. After that, I begin to experiment myself." And he says, "That is my magic." I would only pass that on to people who I think have the moral fiber to hold that knowledge. One which is like intellectual property, his village's heritage, the other personal, patented.

Do you believe that African traditional medicine has special healing qualities?

Yes. Vast pharmacological knowledge, which needs to be researched. I suppose to conclude with that is like a metaphor for what informs my life, that when you go to traditional African religions, its medicines, traditional healing methods, traditional African philosophy and psychology and so on, a lot came direct from the observation of nature and a respect for nature's sacredness. From this we learn about reciprocal altruism, and symbiotic relationships. So, you will have a tree and ants protect the tree from predators and the tree accommodates that. If the ants eat too much of the leaves it will kill the tree, so the tree can send out chemical signals to its ally, some wasps. The wasps will come and control the population of ants, by feeding on the pupae. So, you have to find a model of how it is done in nature, because in nature there's no final oppressor. Each finds a niche, an accommodation. You can find models and paradigms in nature of how to have shifting alliances and so forth, models of how to harvest peace.

What would be your final word to African-Americans?

Study science. Wade Davis for example, he was an ethnobotanist, and he went to study in Haiti about the pufferfish. What makes zombies, and he discovered that they use a fish which is a source of tetradoxin. If it gets in your system, it will stop your heart for seventy-two hours, so they can bury you. That's why the notion that you're a zombie. And then they use Datura to revive you. The thing is that doctors, Western doctors, declare people dead. Understanding that the West didn't know that this was a source of tetradoxin. Of course, you can see medically this is very important for heart surgery and stuff like that. The value of Wade Davis's work is he's a scientist. He had to be initiated. He said this is knowledge in Haiti passed down through secret societies, or rather societies with secrets. Let's tell the children, for God's sakes, stop the "gangsta" rap business and this foolishness, and go and be scientists, emulate Washington and Drew and people like that. There is a contribution you can really, really make. There is real knowledge there to be researched and propagated—challenging intellectual frontiers of the twenty-first century. Be there!

5

African-Americans Who Returned to the United States

Some repatriates returned to the United States for a variety of reasons. For some it was to see family, for others, it was for medical reasons or financial ones. In all cases, the return was for a particular reason and was for a limited period of time. They all were determined to return to Africa and to resume their lives on the continent.

ISMAIL M'BACKE[1]
FEBRUARY 1, 1999

What's your name, and could you, like, spell your name please?
    I-S-M-A-I-L

Is there a last name?
    M-B-A-C-K-E, apostrophe B-A-C-K-E, M'Backe.

Where were you born, Ismail?
    Bronx, New York.

How long did you live in the Bronx?
    I lived in the Bronx twelve years, then we moved to Teaneck, New Jersey, where I lived for another thirteen or fourteen years.

At some point you decided to go to Africa?
    Yeah. I'd say that my interest in Africa began way back in junior high school.

[1]Name has not been altered.

What year was it that you decided to go to Africa?
   1979.

And before you went to Africa, what kind of work were you doing in the United States?
   I was doing some counseling for adolescent boys, and I was doing some coaching in New York City.

Even though you were doing this kind of good work in New York City, you felt the need to go to Africa, is that right?
   Well, I was kind of actively involved in some nationalist organizations, and Africa was basically at the heart of the nationalist movement back in those days.

What kind of educational level had you completed before you went to Africa?
   I had about three years of college.

And where had you gone to school?
   I went to Turo College in Manhattan, 123rd Street and Lexington Avenue.

When did you first develop an interest in Africa?
   I'd say that was there from an early child, because I got introduced to drumming. I used to drum at the Olatungi Cultural Center on 121st Street. I drummed with Elhaga Kamara on Boston Road in the Bronx. Olatungi was a visiting Nigerian, and he wound up staying here in America, and Lagi was the lead drummer from Le Ballet Africaine who came here during, when they had the World's Fair out at Flushing Meadows in Queens. And I met him back in those days and started taking classes at his drum and dance studio on Boston Road in the Bronx.

Were you married when you decided to go to Africa?
   No, I was separated from my wife.

What country did you decide to go to when you left for Africa?
   The first place that I reached was Ivory Coast. Basically because my brother had gone two years prior to my leaving for Africa, and he had a good contact there for me, and at the time, that was a very inexpensive flight from New York City.

Did you speak French?
   Not until I got there. I mean, I had taken a few French classes in high school, but nothing really to speak of. I found that the children and the overall temperament of the people there, it was pretty easy to pick up the

language. When you're in a situation where you have to, I guess it comes easier.

You say that your brother was an influence in helping you to decide to go to Africa. Would you have made that decision even if your brother hadn't?

Well I'm the oldest. I think I was the one who kind of led everybody into it, and then I just wasn't able to leave at the time, immediately upon wanting to go. It took me several years before I got it together to actually make the trip. But my brother had the finances at the time, and he made a trip. It was a honeymoon for he and his wife. And that's where they went, to Senegal.

So when you got to Ivory Coast, what was it like? What was your first impression when the plane set down in Africa?

I was elated at finally having reached the continent, and I landed in Abidjan, and my destination was the Marche du Cocode. I had my contact, Ari, in the local market, and when I met him, we formed a little partnership and went to the small villages collecting art, and you know, buying it from the artist, and bringing it back to the big cities.

How long were you able to sustain yourself, selling art?

I stayed in Abidjan for about two-and-a-half years. My destination was Senegal, though. And a lot of Senegalese helped me to solidify my place there. I collected some artifacts, pewter, silver, some ancient weapons, swords, hatchets, a lot of Selani jewelry.

So were you traveling by yourself?

Yeah, I was alone.

How did you feel about traveling alone in a foreign country?

For me it was an advantage, because, first of all, as a stranger dressed in African clothing people still suspected that I was an American. It has its advantages if you're trying to stay over there for any length of time.

Right.

While in Mali, and in northern Senegal I visited, particularly in Naisenna, I met some people who were incredible. It blew my mind as well as theirs, that we were really able to connect as brothers. And also, when you're traveling like that and you have to, at any point produce an American, that's the passport that you're carrying, they will try to shake you down. They're going to, first of all, want to know why you're there, you know, and what's your business here, and it's a lot of little extortion going on at borders. If they think you have money, they will hold you up and look through your baggage. They want to shake you down for whatever they can, and the people who traveled with me helped me bypass a lot of that by explaining to the truck driver that we would be delayed if in fact they had to put me through that at different frontiers. So what they did was, the driver always has a helper, so about maybe a half a mile from the frontier, he would stop the vehicle and let me and the helper out, and we would walk around for that half a mile, until he reached the frontier, and went through the necessary paperwork and what not with the rest of the Africans who were on board or whatever they had to, whatever cargo they were carrying, and then he would ride up the road a little bit and pick us up, and we would continue on our way.

You went across the border by foot?
   Yeah, I've done that several times to avoid all of that.

Right.
   Regardless of whether you speak the language, regardless, if there's anything different about you that will attract attention to you, they'll want to investigate, that's their job.

Right.
   And being American, it's not that you're not welcome. It's that you're not, just the fact that their impression of what an American is, they've mostly seen only Caucasian soldiers and a few tourists who come in groups, but rarely do they find one traveling alone dressed in traditional garb. I was a Muslim, and I was a Muslim long before I came to Africa, so I knew the basic format for prayer and for all aspects of Islamic ritual, and therefore people respected me wherever I went, and I was welcome.

Did you find a problem with the food, adjusting to the food when you got there?
   Well there were certain things that I didn't eat. In most places, you're a guest, unless you're eating in restaurants or little, by the side of the road places. You're eating with a family out of one big plate. And you sit around the bowl and you eat from your little portion that's directly in front of you, without reaching in the middle or reaching across, and when you've eaten to your satisfaction, you excuse yourself and get up.

But you never had any problems adjusting to the different flavors, spices, etc.
   Yeah, I've had my share of dysentery and diarrhea and all the rest of that. But after awhile, I think your body adjusts. I don't know at what point I adjusted, but I did.

OK, so you finally make it to Senegal, right?

Right. The point of where I got off the train was in Tuba, which is where I wanted to go.

And so did you know anyone in Senegal?

Yeah. I knew the family of, well I had a contact in Dakar but I didn't get to Dakar until about eight months later from when I arrived in Senegal. I arrived about 150 miles north of Dakar, and at that time I was out of money, and I was pretty much in the hands of my hosts, the people that I was supposed to meet when I got there. Who were there, in fact, to meet me when I got off the train. And they took me to their house, which was in a city called Doudell, about twenty-five miles south of Tuba, and I lived there. They had a room prepared for me and everything. I ate with the family, and did my little research and my little writings and they had a little terra cotta school within walking distance from where I was, and I used to go there, and that's where I—between the children in that family and the Islamic school—I kind of got my Wolof, the language of Senegal. I got that kind of tight, before I even got to Dakar.

So how long did you stay in Dakar?

I stayed in Dakar, well, Dakar became my headquarters. I came and went to Mali again, to Guinea, to Gambia. I ran my tours from Senegal. I'm from Dakar. I met my contact person, Abubaka, and we did a lot of tourism endeavors together. I lived with a family in Dakar with Abubaka. His adopted family became my adopted family, and I think I stayed at that house for about a year, until I was able to save enough money to rent my own little room further down, midtown Dakar, called Medina. I lived, I think it was Ruons in Medina, which is in the middle of the heart of Dakar. My rent was like, $25 a month, in American money. Meals were about $1.50.

Now, you said that you had your host family in Dakar. Were they hospitable?

Oh, extremely. The word *taranga* in Wolof means hospitality, and it's the trademark of Senegal. It's one of the most hospitable countries that I visited. I mean, they'll take you in, no questions asked. And to be a stranger is to be the guest of honor, and that's regardless of race or creed or whatever. Had I been a White Christian, they still would've given me the same reception. The fact that I was an African-American Muslim I think was the icing on the cake for me. I mean, I was really the guest of honor. I mean, I met the president, I met the Khalifia of all three of the major Islamic Tarikas in Senegal, I spoke at the Islamic conference. It was really the highest point of my African experience, was Senegal. And I visited maybe ten, eleven countries, but Senegal was the one.

Did you live in the country or in the city?

I lived in both. When I first arrived, I lived in the country. And I think that was good for me, because when I got to Dakar, the language started to become more mixed with French, the closer you get to the big cities. So having lived in Ivory Coast, I could already speak French enough to communicate pretty well, and by the time I left Tuba and Jubel, to get down to Dakar, I was pretty fluent in Wolof. And that helped me considerably when I got down to Dakar because that's where the hub of industry and business and trading and tourism, most of that, the heart of it is in Dakar. Being an African-American, and from New York City, flatfoot hustling was not really a problem for me.

But what probably was an adjustment for you was being in the countryside and being in a completely different world, but you were able to do that. What helped you to adjust to the countryside?

Actually, the country was a lot easier than the city. Because, first of all, the entire structure of Senegal is based around the religion of Islam. So you have, you wake up at sunrise, you make a congregational prayer with either the family you're living in, and I lived about three blocks from a famous mosque, so I could walk there. There's more blessings praying in the mosque than there is praying at home, so the fact that I was praying regularly, and I was a stranger, really opened up a lot of doors for me. The fact that my interest was basically a spiritual pursuit, made them even more interested in me as a person, that there was nothing commercial about living in the country. The people basically had nothing, but they shared everything. The main crop was peanuts, and I helped harvest them. I liked the simplicity of living. I liked traditional garb. I liked the fact that people were, for the most part, one for all and all for one, in spite of their ignorance as to what was actually happening to them, in terms of how modernization and all of these foreign countries were feasting upon them. They kind of took it in stride.

So did you find that you had been accepted as a returned brother?

No question. Some places, I would say most places, a lot of places, Bob, I just passed through unnoticed, because after a period of time, I found that that would be to my advantage. And because of my, I look like a Senegalese, and I found a marketplace called Calabenne in Dakar that sold used clothes, and a lot of the well-to-do people would buy really beautiful baizan, flowing grand boubas and Khaffcannes for a particular occasion like Ramadan or Correta, the end of Ramadan, or any of these festivals. And after the festival they would sell them to the used clothes place, and I would go there and buy outfits. Otherwise I couldn't afford to dress like that, but, you know, having a few outfits like that, to make appearances, and have what I wanted to say together, my questions and my proposals, whenever I would meet these important people, all of that helped me. And in Africa it's pretty much who you know and how you carry yourself that opens doors for you. It was controlled by the Marabout and the Tarikas, and the members of the Tarikas were the ones who went out and actually did the harvesting and all the agriculture, and I joined in, and it wasn't a problem at all.

Do you think that the African-Americans are ready to make that kind of transition, the transition that you made?

I think that this is a divine mission. I think it's above and beyond our control. I think that Africa is a special place and that those of us who have, are discerning and clear enough on the overall situation should make it a priority in our lives to make ourselves acquainted with the continent because our collective rate of awakening determines our future. That's for all Africans, at home and abroad.

And do you feel that if a substantial number of Blacks went back to Africa that they would be accepted by the Africans and the African governments?

No question, no question. We have a right to be there. We are descendants of Africa. We didn't choose to come here and therefore, and people, it's being implemented in their school system. They are teaching now who we are and where we are and where we came from and the fact that Africans are all over the world and some of us are not where we are by choice and should therefore be welcome when we come back home. And I received that kind of treatment in most places I traveled. There were a few incidents, you know, got ignorant people everywhere, good and bad, but for the most part I handled it and Allah was with me.

Now while you were there did you feel like an African, an African-American, or an American?

I just, see, for me I think that we're all integral parts of each other, man, that, you know, I don't really, I didn't, I was an African when I was in Africa because I was forced to live every aspect of it, you know, from sun up to sun down. I mean, even if I wanted to, my situation there would not allow me to, you know, to ostracize myself or to feel any differently. I had to throw down with everybody else, man, put, you know, you know, there were times when I washed up in the stream and, you know, drank from, you know, same place everybody else was drinking from. No matter where I was from, I had, I felt like I was right there with everybody else and I feel that situations and circumstance bring about a common denominator, you know. It makes people see how really alike and we really are, you know, the basic things are so clear in Africa. Things you learn first how to say, you know, I'm hungry, I'm sleepy, where's the bathroom, give me water, you know, everybody will be able to say that in whatever language they need to speak it in, you'll get those phrases together quick.

Now when you were working there, did you make an excellent, good, fair, or poor living?

I made a decent living based on the fact that I'm multidimensional. That was my advantage over them. As I told you before, Africans live like a semi-caste system. If a person's father was a blacksmith, his son will be a blacksmith and they perfect and stay with blacksmithing. Whereas me, I was buying wholesale, selling retail, taking advantage of the fact that I could, you know, was not intimidated at all by White people or anybody else, for that matter. And stepping up to whatever the situation, you know, I had a coffee stand going on. Abubaka and myself had a little spot with a tour agency in Senegal that had a telex and a phone number and what not and people would call us from America that had heard about us. Other African-Americans would go back, would come back to America and tell their friends about us and, you know, make sure that when people go to Africa, to Dakar, they look up Ismail and Abubaka, you know. They can cut to the chase, you ain't got to worry about nothing. If you meet them you know you safe. I mean, I hosted the national council on Negro women. A lot of people who were a little uppity in terms of their expectations about Africa, "You call this air conditioning?" and "Where's the ice water?" and, you know, "It's too hot." I used to tell them, look, if you wanted the Bahamas, you should have went to the Bahamas. This is Africa, that's how it is here. I mean, you know, you didn't have to come on this tour, you can, in fact to-morrow we'll take you back to the hotel and you can stay there! And then again I met people. Like they had the jazz fest in Dakar and I think it was in '85 or '86 when I met Big Black, the drummer. Yeah, I met Roy Haynes. I met Ron Carter, lots of musicians came over there, Billy Higgins, Billy Henderson, lot of, lot of musicians. And some of them, Billy Higgins in particular, I remember he was a Muslim, Abdul Kareem, and he just put his whole life in my hands. He said, "Look, man, we here for two weeks," he said, "I don't know about nobody else, but let's go," you know. He had time and I took him deep into Senegal. I took him to Kasemas, took him to Tuba, Jarim, Tiavorone, Kaolack, I took him to all the holy places, all the places where people could give him readings and give him medicines and places where the, traditionally if you go there just for arriving you blessed, you know, there's a lot of places like that in Senegal and in West Africa. And I met people like that who when they were leaving left me their camera equipment, gave me the rest of their American money, you know, and really hit me off and showed me love and appreciation. Then on the other hand I met some that left me the rest of their toothpaste, you got those kind too.

You mentioned this holy place. Can you elaborate on that a little bit more? What do you mean by holy places?

OK, for example, Amadou Bamba. This man was one of the strongest and most renowned in West Africa because the French wound up giving him back his freedom, his land and everything because they couldn't stop the flow of followers who were coming to him. It just was growing and growing and growing and all their attempts at trying to develop double agents and people to work for them failed and they wound up giving him back his land. He had written some seven tons of prose, poetry in Koranic Arabic and buried some outside strategic places and they exiled him to Gabon and tried to kill him several times and he always survived all of that. The stories are very miraculous and some of them outrageous, but you have generations of Senegalese who believe it all. And it made them band together and faith is works. We can work magic with faith, our people, because we, you know, I've never seen people have so little and do so much with it, you know. It was such a lesson to learn from that, and then to come back here where we just waste and take for granted and just, it's a whole other world.

Well, that gets to my next question. What do you envision the future of African-Americans to be in this country?

I think some of us will completely become absorbed into the American mainstream and be satisfied with that. And I think there will always be a handful or remnant that will try to get home and help and select Africa as an environmental alternative to this, for whatever reasons.

And what do you envision the future of Africa to be?

Now, living in Dakar required a little more ingenuity, because the life-style becomes closer to how I grew up here in America. I mean, everybody's out trying to get a dollar. The money's there, so people are more competitive You've got to watch your back a little more. You've got thieves and hustlers just like in every other big city in the world.

So you mentioned something about being on a spiritual quest. Was that the primary reason why you went to Africa, in search of some kind of spiritual quest?

Yeah, and also just an environmental alternative to this. I had read Garvey, and Amilcar Cabral and Nkrumah. I read everybody before I had gone to Africa, and I think that African-Americans play a great role in the future of Africa, because of our exposure to different technologies, the fact that our proximity to the colonialists puts us at a greater understanding of what is actually happening on the continent, and why. Many different reasons I think, we play a vital role in the development of Africa.

Now, did you meet many other African-Americans there who had decided to move to Africa?

No, I met very few in fact. I'd say, in nine years, I might've met five or six who were serious about it. I met quite a few people who admired the fact that Abubaka and myself, a couple of other brothers that they had met in other countries, had stayed and were making a go of it, but it's not easy. And the adjustment from having whatever you want whenever you want it, to having what you need when the Lord gives it to you is, it's quite an adjustment for the average person. I would say that 90% of the tourists that I've encountered and had the privilege of hosting, as much as they enjoyed it and loved it, and you know, were taken back to the trip to Goree and all of that, they were pretty ready to get back home by the time the tour was over. Because it's not easy.

Now, about being in Africa, what did you miss most about America?

I missed my family, that's all I missed. Because I wanted, I would have loved everybody, my family in particular, all my friends and acquaintances, people that I had been in the struggle with, to share that with me, and see and experience what I was seeing and experiencing. Because it was a mystical journey for me. And it was the proof of all my suspicions before I had arrived in Africa. It was like a dream come true. Even bad things that happened, the sicknesses, the inconveniences, you know, it all balanced out for the good for me.

How did you feel about being there?

I felt that I uncovered a whole lot of what we were missing in our everyday lives, by abandoning our culture and our original lifestyle. As I said before, so many places I visited, the people had absolutely nothing, compared to what I've seen, but they shared everything. And then to come back to America where people have everything and share nothing, it's quite a paradox.

Now, while you were in Africa, did you come back to the States to visit, or did you stay there for a long period of time?

I stayed there until I came back.

OK, so you got there—

And I stayed. And I came back when I got real sick and my brother and a childhood friend came and got me, and went to Guinea, Conakry to visit some friends from Le Ballet Africaine. We stayed about a month there, and then caught the plane back to Dakar, from Dakar to New York.

So if you hadn't gotten sick, you would have stayed there?

Yeah, because I felt, there was a point at which I knew my family wanted me to come back. But I also knew that if I was healthy, and could really set up something there, that because I was the oldest son, and pretty much the catalyst in my community, New York and New Jersey, to expose the culture to a lot of African-Americans, even before I came to Africa, that if I stayed there, maybe I could attract more of them to come and help me set something up there. Because that's really what I want to do. I still want to do that.

How long were you in Africa?

Eight years and ten months.

How long have you been back?

I've been back ten years.

Now did you find that coming from America was an advantage or disadvantage in terms of how you were received?

I found it was an advantage because, I mean, these people are basically uneducated in terms of, I mean, in big cities you find people who are educated and who have learned geography and history and things like that. But I encountered people who were so taken aback by the fact that I was an African-American, a descendant of slaves who had been taken from Africa, that it, they broke down and cried and really, you know, went into depth with me about it and took me as a son, as a lost son and that was too much, man, that was something that words can't describe actually.

Now you mentioned that one of the things that you missed in America was your family. Did you develop a family in Africa?

Several families in Africa, definitely. I have a son that was born by a Senegalese wife and I have a son from my marriage here in America who is involved in an exchange program in Africa and he's been there for six years. He's seventeen years old now.

Oh, I see. Is he in Dakar?

No, he's in Tuba where I got off the train when I first arrived.

One person I interviewed spoke to me about how happy he was coming to Africa and seeing Blacks in positions of authority in banks, Black police-

*men, the whole thing. To him that was the most rewarding thing about being
in Africa. Then on the other hand you could hear people say that that's un-
important because the economic control in Africa is still by foreigners. Do
you have any views on that and did you run into that while you were there?*

Definitely. I still stand firm in the fact that, as long as the yardstick for
success and for power and for respect is how well we can imitate the colonials or the white man, I think that we still are in need of revision. We still need
to redefine our sense of values. We need to redefine our purpose on this
planet because, from my vantage point, I see us as the life givers of this
planet, the people who are really the healers and we're still getting played
out of pocket because they hold the reward over our heads like the carrot on
the stick and those of us who fall for it become puppets in the game and they
use these puppets to manipulate and control the masses of people. Now the
difference in Senegal was that the colonialists pretty much gave up trying to
completely control Senegal through economics or through missionaries
and things like that because they saw that that was not going to work. They
saw that all their attempts at trying to convert these people to Christianity
was not going to be the way. They had to come up with another plan in Senegal because the people there do not think that ties and suits and Tommy Hil-
figer etc., that's not their code of, that's not their dress code. They don't see
that as being clean. For them they dress traditionally and have maintained
that, when they get dressed up they get dressed up traditionally. Now the
people who are wearing western wool in 120 degrees and choked up in
shirts and ties are usually pawns in the game who get a check every month
but for the most part have abandoned their tradition and their culture and
who have traveled to France and who speak French better than French people and who have another sense of values now. I think there's a midway
point that's healthy and an extreme that's dangerous. So I think that's where
we come in. We can, we can help bridge the gap and answer questions for
them and help them become somewhat more self-sufficient and stop beg-
ging.

*So I assume that when you were there you didn't really have much contact or
relationships with the quote unquote African elites.*

No, I didn't. I had, I had, well, in Senegal the African elites are the religious leaders and I had big contact with them. They have more power than the
government officials, even the president, because, for example, in Senegal
one of the largest Mouridene who are followers of a particular sect, his
name was Cheikh Amadou Bamba, who was the major resistant to colonialism in the history of West Africa and who basically thwarted their efforts
peacefully, mystically. All kinds of fables and stories have developed

through his lineage and his family and to this day they control most of the importation of the peanuts which is their major cash crop and also all of the transportation by road over land. And, for example, every year they have a celebration of the return from exile of Cheikh Arubamba's called the Magal into Tuba and every year the numbers go up. At last count it's something like seven, eight million people go to Tuba for this little pilgrimage. And during those two days the transportation thing is sewed up, I mean, nothing moving coming or going unless it's going to Tuba. And while I was there in Senegal they had an Islamic conference where delegations from Libya, from Egypt, from Saudi, all of them came there and it was, it was, it was a strong experience for me because although I have my qualms about certain aspects of ritual in any religion, I've found that Islam, particularly in West Africa, is the most unifying factor that they have. And I would hate to see it without Islam because it's united a lot of warring tribes, and people who were, who had more heavily populated villages would raid smaller villages and, you know, those days are over and I would, I would attribute that to El Hajj Umar and El Hajj Malik and Cheikh Amadou Bamba when they came to promote Islam in that part of Senegal. That's a lot of Africa.

All right. Some Blacks argue that Black people can progress if they get political power. Do you share that belief? Africans have political power, but have they progressed?

I think that they have progressed in some ways and they've stayed the same in many ways and I think that the political power is a sham because the people in power are really puppets for colonial powers abroad.

You're saying that political power is not sufficient.

I think that education and communication amongst the countries would be the answer. I remember some friends of mine who are a little bit older had gone to Ghana back in the days when Kwame Nkrumah was alive and, you know, Accra was headquarters for any and everything that you would want and need in the way of foodstuffs or supplies or traditional medicines, anything. Other tribes and other countries would freely come and go and trade and then, with the politics and the death of prominent leaders, with some puppet type leaders taking control, I think that a lot was lost and everybody started, survival became more difficult. They have been not as cooperative as they used to be, particularly trading with one another and looking out for one another. I think that each country is exclusive unto themselves and they're trying to develop themselves as opposed to trying to develop the continent on a whole, that's something that I think that African-Americans and other Africans who have traveled can see as being counter-productive. Most of them who are not educated, their little world is just their village and where they, place where they wake up every morning. And I think that education would play a great role in the development of Africa, to draw for them the larger picture and to let them know what really is going on. They might have different ideas in terms of how to survive into the next century.

Now in terms of Africa consciousness for African-Americans, how important do you think that is?

I think it's very important because, for two reasons: number one, the sense of pride and dignity and clarity that I received from traveling in Africa. I don't think anything, any kind of formal education here in America could parallel that. And at the same time to travel is an education in itself, I mean, there's nothing like it. I mean, you could read it in a book and you can see it on TV, but to actually experience it, it's no comparison.

How many African countries have you visited?

OK, let me count them. I've been to Ivory Coast, Ghana, Senegal, Gambia, Mali, Niger, Mauritania, and to Nigeria. I'd say about ten or eleven.

That's a lot. And of those, which one do you like the best?

Senegal, Senegambia, no question. I'm home there! You drop me off with nothing, I'm safe.

So do you think that a substantial number of Black Americans should go to Africa to settle?

I'd love it, but I don't see it happening. I met some Black Israelites that were passing through on their way to Tel Aviv. I don't know why they wound up in Africa but I think they had some little scam going. But I also met some Rastafarians that were on their way to Shashumani in Ethiopia. I met some other nationalist groups that were trying to settle in Tanzania. I met a few individual, a couple of, I met two families, a brother and his wife and their two children that had, were living in Ghana. I know sisters who have married Africans and have moved back to Africa but who had, you know, they had a home in America too. They were going back and forth. But I would love to see more African-Americans bridging that gap. I pretty much see Africa as being a place where the whole world will be able to come and become enriched and hopefully as Africans become a little more educated and in control of their own destiny, able to trade more openly with the free world without being taken advantage of and develop themselves and able to exist on a different level.

And you think that African-Americans can help by going back?

Yeah, because we see the big picture clearer and some of us who've become totally involved materially, we can appreciate a break from that when we get it. And it's so simple in Africa that it's an embarrassment when you think of how much time, energy, money, resources that we waste becoming individually attracted to things that don't really make a difference for everybody. I mean, I see it like all we'll ever have is each other and anything other than that is wasting time and energy. So, yeah, I do think that we'll play a definite part in the future of Africa, no question.

Now when you look back on your time in Africa, what long term contribution did you make personally to Africa?

Well, I'll give you an example. Yesterday, in fact, day before yesterday, when Abubaka called me, he told me that he ran into a friend of ours that had made it to America finally in New York. He was a Senegalese, he's a tailor, and he said that people are still talking about he and I there, and that since we've left, there haven't been any people that penetrated the society the way we did. So if nothing else, the mere fact that we stayed long enough to be appreciated and to struggle along with them and show them that we were just like they were in many different aspects and that what we had we shared just like when they had, they shared, I think that made a great impression on a lot of people because the only Americans that they ever saw were soldiers, merchant marines, investors riding around in little minibuses, and that was it. So the fact that, you know, they met two brothers that walked it the way they walked it, shed a light. And I always try to help in any way that I could, on any level that I could, because that's how the people were. They made me feel so at home 'til, I mean, they could have got anything from me.

Looking back on the time when you were there, who stands out or what stands out as the most memorable person or event for you?

Let me think about that one. I think that one of the most memorable events was when I got off the, when I got off the train in Tuba and saw the size of this enormous mosque erected on shifting sand in the middle of the desert, that was so beautiful and so enormous and everybody there was pitch black. There weren't any Arabs there, there weren't any Europeans there, and you could feel the energy, was just too much for me. I, it brought me to tears, I remember that one.

And what country was this in?

That was in Senegal, Tuba.

Now what person had the most impact on how you view the world and Africa? Who influenced you the most in terms of shaping your view of the world and Africa?

There were a lot of people, man. I met Malcolm when I was a kid, he would definitely be one of them. I read Nkrumah. I think Kamara, my drum instructor, he played a great role in my longing to reach the continent as a, when I was young. Reading Garvey, reading Nkrumah, reading Jomo Kenyatta, reading speeches by Sekou Toure and Amilcar Cabral, Patrice Lumumba. I read everything when I was young, and that kind of formed my desire to go. I didn't really know what to expect, you know. I just wanted to go.

Now I have a couple more questions. When you, when you think of Africa now, what do you think of?

I think that I don't want to go back unless I really can come stronger, you know. I want to be able to really do some things and I want to be properly networked with people who feel the way I do about it on this side who, you know, can help me formulate and put into effect certain little projects that could help people there. They're in urgent need of medical supplies and antibiotics, antiseptics, I mean, in addition to their traditional medicine they need to have, they need urgent modern day medical care in a lot of places. That would be one thing. I'd like to play a part in bringing about something huge like that. That is such a powerful thing, man, when Africans come together like that because you see the similarities, how they're interwoven, even the languages, the traditions, the dance, the rhythms, amongst the animist people, their deities, even though they might have different names, they have their equivalent in another language, in another culture that is dealt with the same way. Oh man, there's so many things that can tie it all together if one has the eye to see and that kind of vision.

OK, so it sounds like you're definitely going to go back at some point.

I'd like to die there, brother!

And you'll go back to Senegal?

Oh yeah, I got to go back there, man, you know, I got mad people there, they waiting for me! You know, there's a lot of places I like to go back to, but if I have to set up a headquarters, for me it would be easier in Senegal because they've hosted so many African-Americans and they used to us. They know how we are, they know that we're subject to different things and, you know, I could easily bring African-Americans to Dakar whereas if I was in, for example, Lagos, I couldn't. I couldn't do that, it's too, it's too raw, it's too dangerous, you know I wouldn't want to be responsible for a group of

African-Americans, one or two wandering off by night in Lagos. They might not come back, you know, whereas in Dakar, I got people there, if I say, listen, you can stay with this family for the complete experience, you're safe here and they'll see the kids and everybody, you know, it's a whole different thing.

So is there a point you would like to make on the whole issue of repatriation, Blacks going back to Africa and whether it should happen?

I would say Blacks owe it to themselves and their posterity to make themselves acquainted with Africa and to get there by any means necessary, to reinforce their belief in this blackness, that'll be the icing on the cake for you. If you had any doubts they'll be eliminated once you go to Africa. It was the most rewarding experience of my adult life.

6

Conclusions

Repatriation in the nineteenth century, a product of the American Colonization Society, represented but another form of political and economic imperialism. As with other forms of imperialist expansion, such as that of the British colonists into America, India, Africa, and Latin America, the explicit rationale revolved around the so-called inferiority of the colonized and the implicit obligation of the colonizer to bring civilization and culture. Although the real intentions of the colonizers were usually of an economic nature, such humanitarian rhetoric served to divert attention from the real issue of exploitation. Paul Cuffe preceded the Society, and John Brown Russwurm embraced its resources as a means to accomplish his repatriation goals. Bishop Henry McNeal Turner's nationalist views recognized that for Blacks to be free, they must control their own institutions and repatriate to Africa. More importantly, he placed a major Black institution, the African Methodist Episcopal Church, in the forefront of the repatriation movement of the latter part of the nineteenth century and early twentieth century. As the movement swept into the twentieth century, it was under Black leadership and designed to address the myriad social issues that Blacks faced in America.

In the early twentieth century, the movement was driven by a deep sense of futility among the masses. The Marcus Garvey Movement provided an alternative to the widespread lynching and denial of opportunities that flourished during the Jim Crow Era, which sprang into existence after the ratification of the post–Civil War amendments and continued until the U.S. Supreme Court decision of *Brown v. Board of Education* (1954).

The interviews in this volume cover a historical period in America when Blacks struggled to achieve civil rights and Black power. It was a tumultuous time that witnessed the assassination of many Black leaders (Malcolm X, Dr. Martin Luther King Jr., Medgar Evers, Fred Hampton), and the Vietnam War that drafted Black men off the streets and placed them on the front lines in Asia.

Each of the repatriates in this study had acquired a college education. Some had even obtained advanced academic degrees. Despite these academic achievements, they did not believe that America could provide the type of fulfillment that was essential to human development.

Over and over again, the individuals referred to racism as the major obstacle to personal satisfaction. Several had lived in Europe for years and felt that racism in the United States was more virulent. Yet they still did not resettle in Europe. The choice of Africa indicated a desire not only to leave America, but also to avoid all other European nations. It is interesting that though these individuals endorsed repatriation for themselves, they were cautious about mass repatriation. This sentiment most distinguished this group from the Marcus Garvey Movement. Garveyites saw repatriation as a means to achieve national autonomy for African people. Moreover, it was a movement that would empower African people the world over. Although the individuals of this book made very personal decisions, most seemed unaware that their actions were rooted in a rich historical continuum.

Increasingly, consciousness of Africa is becoming a part of the African-American worldview. Throughout the nation, academics have established departments that have Africa and the diaspora as the center of academic inquiry. In addition, political and social movements in Africa, particularly in South Africa and Zaire, have focused worldwide attention upon the continent. These current events underline the fact that though tremendous strides have been made to create a productive and egalitarian environment in Africa, much needs to be done.

What forces and factors will most likely advance the repatriation debate into the twenty-first century? In the nineteenth century, the major social factor was slavery. In the twentieth century, it was lynching, Jim Crowism, and the desire for Black power. In the twenty-first century, the deteriorating socioeconomic condition of the Black masses will, in all likelihood, be the predominant factor that will propel nationalist discussions toward repatriation. Although over the past three decades a significant number of Blacks have entered the middle class, the lives of the vast majority of Blacks have deteriorated. This phenomenon has been ably documented by scholars such as Manning Marable and Julius Wilson.

The effort to bring repatriation to the center stage of the debate will not be easy. The idea of repatriation has yet to be fully accepted by Black intellectuals, and there is little reason to believe that a massive repatriation plan would meet with any success among mainstream White politicians and business people. However, scholars, who acknowledge the legitimacy of the concept, can increasingly raise the question in their conferences and journals. But they must also bring the debate to the Black communities of America, among the poor who struggle daily for survival.

The Black masses may have little, in terms of material wealth, but they, for the most part, have enduring relationships with Black institutions. Scholars must reach out to these institutions and become involved. Many religious institutions, both Moslem and Christian, will continue to be most connected with those who suffer at the bottom of the American social strata. As with the African Methodist Episcopal Church of the nineteenth century, other Christian churches and the Nation of Islam will seek means to alleviate the overwhelming misery that forms the social underpinnings of poverty and despair. Those scholars who are able to synthesize their scholarship on repatriation with the needs of the poorest of the African-American community should be able to shape a debate that gives due credit to an aspect of the Black social movement that has received too little attention.

Bibliography

Angell, Stephen Ward. *Bishop Henry McNeal Turner and African-American Religion in the South.* Knoxville: University of Tennessee Press, 1992.

Franklin, John Hope. *From Slavery to Freedom*: *A History of Negro Americans.* 3rd Edition. New York: Alfred A. Knopf. 1967.

Garvey, Amy Jacques. *The Philosophy and Opinions of Marcus Garvey, Vols. I and II.* New York: Atheneum Press, 1970.

Ginzberg, Eli, and Alfred S. Eichner. *The Troublesome Presence.* New York: Mentor Book, 1964.

Harris, Sheldon H. *Paul Cuffe: Black America and African Return.* New York: Simon and Schuster, 1972.

Johnson, Robert Jr. *Returning Home*: *A Century of African-American Repatriation.* Unpublished.

Martin, Tony. *Race First.* Dover, Mass.: Majority Press, 1976.

National Archives of Jamaica. "Register of Baptisms, Parish of Portland." Spanish Town, Jamaica, 1799.

Redley, Edwin S. *Black Exodus*: *Black Nationalist and the Back to Africa Movements, 1890–1910.* New Haven: Yale University Press, 1969.

Rotberg, Robert I. *A Political History of Tropical Africa.* New York: Harcourt, Brace and World, 1965.

Index

About the Author

ROBERT JOHNSON, JR. is a published playwright, attorney, and professor of Africana Studies at the University of Massachusetts at Boston. He is the author of numerous plays, has published widely in journals, and is the author of *Race, Law and Public Policy.*

ISBN 0-275-96595-3

EAN

HARDCOVER BAR CODE

DATE DUE

			Printed in USA

HIGHSMITH #45230